LUCRETIA MOTT

LUCRETIA MOTT

Gina De Angelis

CHELSEA HOUSE PUBLISHERS
PHILADELPHIA

Frontispiece: In the U.S. Capitol Rotunda stands a marble sculpture memorializing three activists in the women's rights movement of 19th century America: (from left to right) Elizabeth Cady Stanton, Susan B. Anthony, and Lucretia Mott.

Chelsea House Publishers
EDITOR IN CHIEF Stephen Reginald
PRODUCTION MANAGER Pamela Loos
ART DIRECTOR Sara Davis
DIRECTOR OF PHOTOGRAPHY Judy L. Hasday
MANAGING EDITOR James D. Gallagher
SENIOR PRODUCTION EDITOR J. Christopher Higgins

Staff for **Lucretia Mott**
SENIOR EDITOR LeeAnne Gelletly
EDITORIAL ASSISTANT Rob Quinn
ASSOCIATE ART DIRECTOR Takeshi Takahashi
DESIGNER Emiliano Begnardi
PICTURE RESEARCHER Sandy Jones
COVER DESIGNER Keith Trego

The Chelsea House World Wide Web address is
http://www.chelseahouse.com

First Printing
1 3 5 7 9 8 6 4 2

Library of Congress Cataloging-in-Publication Data

De Angelis, Gina.
Lucretia Mott / Gina De Angelis.
    p. cm. — (Women of achievement)
Includes bibliographical references and index.
ISBN 0-7910-5295-8 — ISBN 0-7910-5296-6 (pbk.)
1. Mott, Lucretia, 1793–1880—Juvenile literature. 2. Feminists—United States—Biography—Juvenile literature. 3. Women abolitionists—United States — Biography —Juvenile literature. 4. Quakers —United States — Biography — Juvenile literature. [1. Mott, Lucretia, 1793–1880. 2. Abolitionists. 3. Feminists. 4. Women—Biography.] I. Title. II. Series.

HQ1413.M68 D43 2000
326.8'092—dc21
[B]   00-038375

21.95

CONTENTS

WOMEN OF ACHIEVEMENT

Jane Addams
SOCIAL WORKER

Madeleine Albright
STATESWOMAN

Marian Anderson
SINGER

Susan B. Anthony
WOMAN SUFFRAGIST

Clara Barton
AMERICAN RED CROSS FOUNDER

Margaret Bourke-White
PHOTOGRAPHER

Rachel Carson
BIOLOGIST AND AUTHOR

Cher
SINGER AND ACTRESS

Hillary Rodham Clinton
FIRST LADY AND ATTORNEY

Katie Couric
JOURNALIST

Diana, Princess of Wales
HUMANITARIAN

Emily Dickinson
POET

Elizabeth Dole
POLITICIAN

Amelia Earhart
AVIATOR

Gloria Estefan
SINGER

Jodie Foster
ACTRESS AND DIRECTOR

Betty Friedan
FEMINIST

Althea Gibson
TENNIS CHAMPION

Ruth Bader Ginsburg
SUPREME COURT JUSTICE

Helen Hayes
ACTRESS

Katharine Hepburn
ACTRESS

Mahalia Jackson
GOSPEL SINGER

Helen Keller
HUMANITARIAN

**Ann Landers/
Abigail Van Buren**
COLUMNISTS

Barbara McClintock
BIOLOGIST

Margaret Mead
ANTHROPOLOGIST

Edna St. Vincent Millay
POET

Julia Morgan
ARCHITECT

Toni Morrison
AUTHOR

Grandma Moses
PAINTER

Lucretia Mott
WOMAN SUFFRAGIST

Sandra Day O'Connor
SUPREME COURT JUSTICE

Rosie O'Donnell
ENTERTAINER AND COMEDIAN

Georgia O'Keeffe
PAINTER

Eleanor Roosevelt
DIPLOMAT AND HUMANITARIAN

Wilma Rudolph
CHAMPION ATHLETE

Elizabeth Cady Stanton
WOMAN SUFFRAGIST

Harriet Beecher Stowe
AUTHOR AND ABOLITIONIST

Barbra Streisand
ENTERTAINER

Elizabeth Taylor
ACTRESS AND ACTIVIST

Mother Teresa
HUMANITARIAN AND
RELIGIOUS LEADER

Barbara Walters
JOURNALIST

Edith Wharton
AUTHOR

Phillis Wheatley
POET

Oprah Winfrey
ENTERTAINER

Babe Didrikson Zaharias
CHAMPION ATHLETE

"REMEMBER THE LADIES"

MATINA S. HORNER

"Remember the Ladies." That is what Abigail Adams wrote to her husband John, then a delegate to the Continental Congress, as the Founding Fathers met in Philadelphia to form a new nation in March of 1776. "Be more generous and favorable to them than your ancestors. Do not put such unlimited power in the hands of the Husbands. If particular care and attention is not paid to the Ladies," Abigail Adams warned, "we are determined to foment a Rebellion, and will not hold ourselves bound by any Laws in which we have no voice, or Representation."

The words of Abigail Adams, one of the earliest American advocates of women's rights, were prophetic. Because when we have not "remembered the ladies," they have, by their words and deeds, reminded us so forcefully of the omission that we cannot fail to remember them. For the history of American women is as interesting and varied as the history of our nation as a whole. American women have played an integral part in founding, settling, and building our country. Some we remember as remarkable women who—against great odds—achieved distinction in the public arena: Anne Hutchinson, who in the 17th century became a charismatic religious leader; Phillis Wheatley, an 18th-century black slave who became a poet; Susan B. Anthony, whose name is synonymous with the 19th-century women's rights movement, and who led the struggle to enfranchise women; and in the 20th century, Amelia Earhart, the first woman to cross the Atlantic Ocean by air.

These extraordinary women certainly merit our admiration, but other women, "common women," many of them all but forgotten, should also be recognized for their contributions to American thought and culture. Women have been community builders; they have founded schools and formed voluntary associations to help those in need; they have assumed the major responsibility for rearing children, passing on from one generation to the next the values that keep a culture alive. These and innumerable other contributions, once ignored, are now being recognized by scholars, students, and the public. It is exciting and gratifying that a part of our history that was hardly acknowledged a few generations ago is now being studied and brought to light.

In recent decades, the field of women's history has grown from obscurity to a politically controversial splinter movement to academic respectability, in many cases mainstreamed into such traditional disciplines as history, economics, and psychology. Scholars of women, both female and male, have organized research centers at such prestigious institutions as Wellesley College, Stanford University, and the University of California. Other notable centers for women's studies are the Center for the American Woman and Politics at the Eagleton Institute of Politics at Rutgers University; the Henry A. Murray Research Center for the Study of Lives, at Radcliffe College; and the Women's Research and Education Institute, the research arm of the Congressional Caucus on Women's Issues. Other scholars and public figures have established archives and libraries, such as the Schlesinger Library on the History of Women in America, at Radcliffe College, and the Sophia Smith Collection, at Smith College, to collect and preserve the written and tangible legacies of women.

From the initial donation of the Women's Rights Collection in 1943, the Schlesinger Library grew to encompass vast collections documenting the manifold accomplishments of American women. Simultaneously, the women's movement in general and the academic discipline of women's studies in particular also began with a narrow definition and gradually expanded their mandate. Early causes, such as woman suffrage and social reform, abolition, and organized labor were joined by newer concerns, such as the history of women in business and the professions and in politics and government; the study of the family; and social issues such as health policy and education.

Women, as historian Arthur M. Schlesinger, jr., once pointed out, "have constituted the most spectacular casualty of traditional history. They have made up at least half the human race, but you could never tell that by looking at the books historians write." The new breed of historians is remedying that omission. They have written books about immigrant women and about working-class women who struggled for survival in cities and about black women who met the challenges of life in rural areas. They are telling the stories of women who, despite the barriers of tradition and economics, became lawyers and doctors and public figures.

The women's studies movement has also led scholars to question traditional interpretations of their respective disciplines. For example, the study of war has traditionally been an exercise in military and political analysis, an examination of strategies planned and executed by men. But scholars of women's history have pointed out that wars have also been periods of tremendous change and even opportunity for women, because the very absence of men on the home front enabled them to expand their educational, economic, and professional activities and to assume leadership in their homes.

The early scholars of women's history showed a unique brand of courage in choosing to investigate new subjects and take new approaches to old ones. Often, like their subjects, they endured criticism and even ostracism by their academic colleagues. But their efforts have unquestionably been worthwhile, because with the publication of each new study and book another piece of the historical patchwork is sewn into place, revealing an increasingly comprehensive picture of the role of women in our rich and varied history.

Such books on groups of women are essential, but books that focus on the lives of individuals are equally indispensable. Biographies can be inspirational, offering their readers the example of people with vision who have looked outside themselves for their goals and have often struggled against great obstacles to achieve them. Marian Anderson, for instance, had to overcome racial bigotry in order to perfect her art and perform as a concert singer. Isadora Duncan defied the rules of classical dance to find true artistic freedom. Jane Addams had to break down society's notions of the proper role for women in order to create new social situations, notably the settlement house. All of these women had to come to terms both with themselves and with the world in which they lived. Only then could they move ahead as pioneers in their chosen callings.

Biography can inspire not only by adulation but also by realism. It helps us to see not only the qualities in others that we hope to emulate, but also, perhaps, the weaknesses that made them "human." By helping us identify with the subject on a more personal level they help us feel that we, too, can achieve such goals. We read about Eleanor Roosevelt, for instance, who occupied a unique and seemingly enviable position as the wife of the president. Yet we can sympathize with her inner dilemma; an inherently shy woman, she had to force herself to live a most public life in order to use her position to benefit others. We may not be able to imagine ourselves having the immense poetic talent of Emily Dickinson, but from her story we can understand the challenges faced by a creative woman who was expected to fulfill many family responsibilities. And though few of us will ever reach the level of athletic accomplishment displayed by Wilma Rudolph or Babe Zaharias, we can still appreciate their spirit, their overwhelming will to excel.

A biography is a multifaceted lens. It is first of all a magnification, the intimate examination of one particular life. But at the same time, it is a wide-angle lens, informing us about the world in which the subject lived. We come away from reading about one life knowing more about the social, political, and economic fabric of the time. It is for this reason, perhaps, that the great New England essayist Ralph Waldo Emerson wrote in 1841, "There is properly no history: only biography." And it is also why biography, and particularly women's biography, will continue to fascinate writers and readers alike.

Lucretia Coffin Mott receives a "ruffian's" protection during a women's rights convention. The 19th century Quaker minister spent her life working for a variety of social causes, including abolition (ending slavery) and women's rights, and was familiar with people who were hostile to reform.

1

NANTUCKET HERETIC

The shouts and jeers of hecklers were disrupting the second day of the 1853 women's rights convention at Broadway Tabernacle, New York City, just as they had the day before. The speakers tried to continue, but the taunts became so loud and insistent that no one could be heard. The meeting was hastily adjourned.

A group of toughs, known as the Rynders' Gang, confronted the convention's male speakers: William Lloyd Garrison, a radical abolitionist who was often hanged in effigy throughout the slaveholding South; Henry Highland Garnet, a former slave who had become a minister; and Charles Burleigh, an abolitionist journalist. But even rowdy gangs in 1853 did not go after female speakers—who at this convention included Ernestine Rose, a radical reformer and feminist; Lucy Stone and Susan B. Anthony, women's rights advocates; and a small, 60-year-old woman who was dressed in the plain gray dress and white shawl of the Religious Society of Friends, known as Quakers.

The petite woman saw that the uproar had terrified several other women at the convention. She herself was calm, despite knowing

An early 1800s view of a Nantucket Island village, much like the one in which Lucretia Mott grew up. The town of Nantucket was a close-knit island community, in which families depended on one another while seafaring husbands and fathers were away.

she was a likely target for the mob's rage. She was the uncompromising proponent of the many reform movements of the day. At a time when most people did not approve of women speaking in public, she loudly and continuously advocated the abolition of slavery and the equality of women and men. Many people considered her a religious liberal; others called her a socialist and a heretic (someone who opposes accepted church principles).

The small woman told her escort to help the panicking women safely out of the building. "Then who will escort you?" he asked.

"This man here," she answered, laying her hand on the arm of the gang leader, Capt. Isaiah Rynders. Caught off guard by the grandmotherly figure, Rynders agreed. Once they were safely outside, away from the chaos, the small woman thanked him for his help.

The next day, when she saw the captain in a local restaurant, the Quaker lady struck up a pleasant conversation with him. After the two parted, Rynders asked someone who she was.

"That woman?" must have been the surprised response. "That was Lucretia Mott."

Lucretia Mott? The heretical, rabble-rousing, "uppity" woman? Rynders must have been surprised, but said only, "Well, she seemed like a good, sensible woman."

*   *   *

That "good, sensible woman" had been born 60 years earlier to Thomas and Anna Coffin, on January 3, 1793, on the island of Nantucket, off the southeastern coast of Massachusetts. Lucretia Coffin was their second daughter, and she came from a notable New England family. Its members included several governors, judges, and other officeholders, many of whom pursued more than one trade.

Lucretia's Coffin ancestors were among the first white settlers of Nantucket Island. Some of them were Quakers, members of the Christian religious sect known as the Society of Friends. One ancestor, Vestal Coffin, reportedly founded the Underground Railroad in the 1700s. (The Underground Railroad was a network of safe houses that runaway slaves stayed in as they traveled north to freedom.) Lucretia was also distantly related to John Greenleaf Whittier, a leading poet and Quaker, as well as to Benjamin Franklin, one of the Founding Fathers of the United States.

Lucretia's father, like many men on the island of Nantucket, made his living on the sea. Those who lived on the island could do little else; farming on the sandy soil was difficult, if not impossible. Whaling and trading were the lifeblood of Nantucket. As captain of his own trading ship, Thomas Coffin was often away, sometimes for up to two years at a time. Anna Folger married Thomas when she was 17 years old, but she was no stranger to the seafaring life. She came from a long line of mariners, and she bravely faced the difficulties that came during her husband's absences.

The Coffin family grew with the birth of Eliza in 1794, Thomas Mayhew in 1798, Mary in 1800, and Martha in 1806. (Anna also gave birth to two other children, in 1797 and 1804, both of whom died in infancy.) Lucretia was particularly close to her younger sister Eliza. The two were constant companions in childhood, and later as adults leading separate lives, they would correspond almost daily.

When Lucretia was seven years old, her father, Captain Thomas Coffin, set out on what was to be his last voyage. He was headed for China, to trade sealskins for silks, tea, and other goods. As always, he wrote to his family when he could, but after a year, Anna heard nothing from him. As time went on and no news arrived, the Coffin family concluded that Thomas was probably dead.

During her husband's long absences Anna had always relied on her own abilities to make ends meet. Although at the turn of the 19th century women's prospects were severely limited—married women had no legal rights, were not citizens, and could not hold property or have custody of their children should they leave an abusive husband—Anna was not alone on Nantucket. Many other families on the island were familiar with the difficulties caused by the menfolk's long absences.

When times were hard, Anna would open a shop. Her successful shopkeeping doubtless impressed her daughters, who learned that independence and resourcefulness were necessary virtues. Years later, Lucretia would comment on her mother's self-sufficiency:

> I can remember how our mothers were employed while our
> fathers were at sea. . . . At that time it required some money

and some courage to get to Boston. [The women] were obliged to go to that city, make their trades, exchange their oils and candles for dry goods, and all the varieties of a country store, set their own price, keep their own accounts; and with all this, have very little help in the family to which they must discharge their duties.

Lucretia wasn't the only one who saw that her mother was the equal of any man. Thomas would give his wife Anna the full power of attorney while he was at sea; in other words, Anna was legally allowed to control Thomas's (and her own) property as she saw fit. This may not have been an unusual thing in Nantucket, but it was certainly not typical of most men of the early 19th century.

When Anna ran the shop, her children were expected to help keep up the household. Apparently Lucretia's older sister Sarah was mentally disabled in some way, and so the burden of helping run the household fell on Lucretia's young shoulders when her mother was away purchasing supplies.

Anna Folger Coffin, Lucretia's mother, took charge of home and finances the many times her husband, Thomas, was at sea. To help make ends meet during those times, Anna ran a general store.

Anna relied on all her children to help with the day-to-day family tasks. Typically, the two oldest girls would be up before dawn so that Sarah could tend the younger children while Lucretia fetched water and firewood for breakfast. Lucretia then washed dishes and left for school with her sister Eliza. After school both Lucretia and Eliza hurried home to help Anna mind the store. As author Otelia Cromwell notes, the children learned "not only to become careful housekeepers but to regard good housekeeping with wholesome respect."

Lucretia had much to learn both in and out of school. While the education of the day allowed boys to learn more "serious" subjects than the girls would study, there was equality in other areas of the small Nantucket school. All children learned handwriting and basic mathematics, as well as an appreciation of poetry and literature. Lucretia's school also emphasized piety and morality, and if the parents requested, students could learn sewing and knitting as well. Outside of school, Lucretia and her sisters learned to mind their mother's shop, to mend and darn, to make rugs from scraps of fabric, to make candles, to cook, and to perform other household tasks.

Unlike many other children raised during this period, Lucretia and her siblings were treated with gentleness. They were never harshly punished either at school or at home.

According to Lucretia, she had a wonderful childhood. Throughout her long life she always looked back fondly on her Nantucket days. In her own household she maintained what she called "Nantucket ways" in cooking and housekeeping, and she passed them on to her own children.

Lucretia's family was Quaker. This Protestant faith emphasizes that all people—male, female, white, black—are spiritual equals. Quakers believe that each person has an Inner Light—that God resides in every man's and woman's soul and that every person communicates directly with God. Obedience to one's Inner Light leads to salvation. The doctrine of Inner Light means that each person is responsible for his or her own salvation; spiritual health awaits those who live morally.

Quaker services, called Meetings, are not run by a clergy member. The people sit in silence contemplating God. No one speaks unless the Spirit moves him or her; especially strict Quakers do nothing, in fact, unless the Spirit moves them. If a person—either male or female, a radical notion at the time—speaks well and frequently, the Quaker elders might confer on him or her the title of minister.

Quakers are also pacifists—that is, they do not believe in violence. Obedience to the Inner Light sometimes means defying government laws—without violence, of course. The Inner Light also gives those who resist unjust laws confidence that their actions are morally right.

Because of their beliefs, Quakers made up a disproportionate number in the many reform movements that sprang up in 19th-century America. The first organization in the world to ban slavery, for example, was the Society of Friends in 1775; Nantucket Quakers had opposed slavery as early as 1716. The abolition movement—made up of those who believed in putting an end to slavery—always counted many prominent Quakers among its members.

Even in her earliest years, Lucretia was enraged only by injustice. As a young girl she once saw a woman tied

Lucretia Mott was raised a Quaker, a member of the Religious Society of Friends. She and her family would worship at a Quaker meetinghouse, much like the one shown here.

A scene inside a Pennsylvania Quaker meetinghouse in the 1800s. George Fox founded the Religious Society of Friends around 1652 in England. Its members typically worship in silence, speaking only when so inspired.

to a whipping post and flogged. The event touched her deeply. Years later, when in her eighties and on a visit to Nantucket, she brought her great-granddaughters to the site of the beating. Despite the passage of so many years, her voice still trembled with outrage as she told her great-granddaughters of the cruel event.

The institution of slavery also upset Lucretia at a young age. Her first exposure to slavery was through school class books. Once she read an antislavery book describing the horror of the "Middle Passage," the journey that kidnapped Africans took from their homes to slavery in the New World. She particularly remembered the pictures of the slave ship, crammed with the bodies of far too many people for all to survive.

When Lucretia was 10 years old, three years after Thomas Coffin had left, a ship appeared near the island. As was the custom, the news traveled with remarkable speed. Town criers called out the word; families hurried to the "widow's walks" for a better look. (A widow's walk is an observation platform located on top of coastline houses from which a wife could watch for her sailor husband's return.) Once identified with spyglasses, the ship was greeted by a crowd on the wharf. On board the vessel was Lucretia's father. When Thomas Coffin returned as if from the dead, the entire community rejoiced.

As Captain Coffin explained, about a year into the voyage, his ship had been overtaken by Spaniards off the west coast of South America. First he had been imprisoned. Then he had tried to mount a legal case in the Spanish courts to regain his ship, but to no avail. Although he had written his family, his letters never arrived. At last Thomas decided to make for home, and he walked alone across the Andes Mountains. In a Brazilian port he found a sympathetic countryman who agreed to carry him home.

Captain Coffin's tales of his adventures pleased and excited his young children, who begged him to tell the stories again and again. Seventy years later, Lucretia still recalled the Spanish words and phrases the captain had taught his children.

Life on Nantucket was, for young Lucretia, an endless round of gatherings with both her mother's and her father's relatives. As an adult Lucretia would look back fondly on her early years on the island. As the years passed she would, as was the Nantucket way, keep in touch with cousins, nieces, nephews, in-laws, grandnephews, great-aunts, and everyone else in the Folger-Coffin clan.

Soon after Captain Coffin's return, he decided to leave the seafaring life and become a merchant. This meant the family had to relocate to the mainland. So in 1804 the Coffin family moved to one of the young nation's biggest cities—Boston, Massachusetts.

Thomas Coffin's income was large enough that his children could attend private school in Boston, but he reasoned that it was easier in a private school to develop feelings of pride and superiority over those less fortunate. He wanted his children, instead, to learn "democratic principles" and a more respectful attitude toward others, whatever their social class or standing. Consequently, the Coffin children attended public school in Boston.

When Lucretia turned 13, however, her parents determined that their daughters deserved a better education. The Coffins decided that Nine Partners, a Quaker boarding school located in Dutchess County, New York, was the place to get it. Nine Partners' name honored the nine Quakers who had founded it in 1796. One of the leaders of this school was James Mott Sr., a man renowned for his educational method and solid principles. Unlike many other schools of the day, Nine Partners aimed toward a more equal curriculum for boys and girls, although the two sexes lived and worked in separate areas. Both Lucretia and Eliza attended Nine Partners. Their brother Thomas attended another Quaker school, Westtown, which was located in Pennsylvania.

Because the school ran year round, new students joined any time of the year—whenever they were ready. As Quaker dress was simple and practical, the school required that its students' clothing be very plain and sturdy. The administrator's instructions stated that "if the clothing sent be not plain or require much washing it is to be returned or colored, or altered at the parents' expense."

The strictness of the school extended to discipline as well, although corporal punishment, common in all schools at the time, was against the educational principles of James Mott Sr. and other Quakers. Lucretia remembered a young boy who was punished for some infraction by being locked in a closet. Lucretia and

FRIENDS' BRICK MEETING HOUSE AT NINE PARTNERS.

Elizabeth, tenderhearted souls that they were, found a way to sneak into the boys' side of the school and slide buttered bread under the door to the boy.

At Nine Partners, Lucretia was known for her sparkling personality and serious study habits. During her stay at the school, she was the top student among both boys and girls.

One of Lucretia's friends at Nine Partners, Sarah Mott, invited Lucretia to visit her at her home in Long Island, New York, during a school break. Here Lucretia met a tall, blond, serious young man named James Mott Jr., who was the grandson of one of the school's administrators. Despite differences in their personalities—

At the age of 13, Lucretia Coffin left her family in Boston, Massachusetts, to attend Nine Partners, a Quaker boarding school located in New York State.

This early 1800s woodcut illustrates the simple Quaker clothing of the time. Students attending the Nine Partners school had to pack outfits that were plain and practical; otherwise, families were admonished, the clothing would be "returned or colored, or altered at the parents' expense."

Lucretia was lively and outgoing, while James was quiet—a friendship blossomed between the two young people.

James, although only 17 years old, became a teacher on the boys' side at Nine Partners; in fact, he was the senior teacher. Lucretia, in turn, finished her studies in 1808, when she was only 15. As was usual in the year-round school, there was no formal graduation. One simply completed the required curriculum and went home. But Lucretia, as the best student in the school, was asked to stay. She was offered an assistant teaching position, helping Deborah Rogers, who taught reading, grammar, and arithmetic to nearly 60 students. The post offered no salary at first, but loving school as she did, she accepted.

As a teaching assistant, Lucretia found herself in a more liberal world than the one she had lived in as a student. The teachers and staff members were friendly and thoughtful. They loved learning just as Lucretia did. They formed a small class to learn French, and during these study sessions Lucretia and James's friendship grew even closer.

Lucretia did not mind working for no salary, but one thing did bother her, and she would talk about it for years to come: women and men at Nine Partners did not receive equivalent salaries. Deborah Rogers, an experienced and knowledgeable teacher, earned a salary of about $20 a year. Meanwhile, the superintendent (principal) of the school received $150, and James Mott Jr., despite his age and inexperience, received a salary of $100. It was quite common for women to be paid less than men, even when performing the same work. This was an injustice Lucretia would never forget.

Lucretia left Nine Partners in 1810, when she was 17. Soon afterward, the Coffin family moved to Philadelphia, Pennsylvania, then the largest city in the United States. Compared to Boston, Philadelphia had a much friendlier attitude toward Quakers; after all, the city had been founded by the Quaker William Penn. Thomas Coffin owned a factory outside the city that manufactured cut nails. He had bought it before he moved his family, and the business was doing well.

When Lucretia returned to her family, she met her newest sister, Martha, who had been born while Lucretia was away at school. Her sisters Eliza and Mary were entering the nearby Quaker school of Westtown, which Lucretia's brother Thomas had attended.

Soon Thomas Coffin needed help running his business, and he offered a position to James Mott Jr. Both the Coffins and the Motts heartily approved of Lucretia and James's close friendship. In April 1811 the two were married in a simple Quaker ceremony in Philadelphia, and they began a new life together.

Lucretia Mott's family moved to Philadelphia in 1810 and became active partici-pants in its large Quaker community. Lucretia would spend most of her life attending Race Street Meeting House, shown here.

2

INSPIRED TO ACT

For the first few months of their married life Lucretia and James lived at the Coffin house, but in August 1811 they set up their own home nearby on Union Street. By all accounts theirs was a particularly good marriage. Although Lucretia was small, quick, and vivacious, and James was tall, sober, and quiet, the two formed a strong partnership that was noticeably more equal than many marriages at the time. In August 1812 Lucretia gave birth to her first child, Anna.

Only 18 years old, Lucretia already displayed great strength of character, and she was not afraid to go against accepted practices. Although women were normally confined to the bedroom for several weeks after the birth of a child, Lucretia was seen riding in a carriage just one week after Anna's birth. The staid, somber Quakers of Philadelphia were shocked, and as Lucretia later recalled, she was "classified among the Indians for so rash an act." Similarly, she did not hire a nurse for her baby as many wives did. It was not the Nantucket way, and besides, she thought it was a waste of money.

Thomas Coffin Sr.'s nail-manufacturing business began to falter at this time. The Napoleonic wars in Europe and the War of 1812 between the United States and Britain had disrupted trade. In need of work, James Mott moved his family to his parents' home in Mamaroneck, New York. There Lucretia had her second child, Thomas Coffin Mott, in July 1814. Her husband worked at his uncle's cotton mill, until the British blockade affected the cotton trade so badly that the uncle could no longer afford to pay his workers. The Motts then returned to Philadelphia, where they again moved in with Lucretia's parents in late 1814.

Shortly after that, Lucretia's sister Eliza married Benjamin Yarnell, a man from a prominent Philadelphia Quaker family. Meanwhile, Thomas Coffin Sr. had become heavily indebted due to a loan that he had made to a friend—against his wife's advice—and was forced to sell his business. His financial failure scandalized the prominent Quakers of Philadelphia.

Life grew even worse for the Coffins. Thomas Sr. fell ill in early 1815 and died. Yet again, Lucretia's mother rose to the challenge of supporting her children on her own. She opened up a store, and later she would also run a boardinghouse.

James, too, opened a store, but he did not have Anna's talent for business, and he was soon forced to close. Lucretia encouraged him to take a bank clerk job in New York. Then Lucretia herself decided to help out. Instead of following her husband to New York, she took a teaching job at a Quaker school with Rebecca Bunker, a relative of her mother's. While she was there, she learned of a job for James that was available in Philadelphia. Never one to refuse wise advice, particularly from his wife, James returned to the city.

In April 1817 both Lucretia and her young son, Thomas, fell ill. The boy never recovered. Although this was not the first death of a loved one Lucretia had experienced (both her father and two young sisters had already died), the loss of her child plunged her into a

The son of a British aristocrat, William Penn (1644–1718) converted to the Quaker faith in 1667, and was imprisoned repeatedly for his convictions. Lucretia Mott often studied Penn's writings and would quote him when she spoke at Meetings.

spiritual search. Her faith in God was never shaken, but she disputed the idea that God's ways were mysterious. She did not believe God could be cruel or unjust, or that good ever came out of evil. She decided that human error, not God's will, resulted in tragedies like her son's death—and in other wrongs like slavery and the subjugation of women, as well.

In 1818 Lucretia had another daughter, Maria. Even when busy with her young children and other concerns, however, Lucretia always found time to read. Unlike many women of her day, she never read novels; she was much more interested in serious works and particularly in religion. Now she began reading the writings of

The Westtown School, in Chester County, Pennsylvania, educated many members of Lucretia Mott's Quaker family, including her brother and sisters, as well as her children.

William Ellery Channing, who had founded the Unitarian Church in the United States. Lucretia pondered deeply over spiritual matters, and in 1818, about a year after her son's death, she rose to speak in Meeting for the first time.

As Lucretia's Inner Light directed her to speak at more Meetings, she developed a talent for speaking fearlessly, relying on her own intelligence as she quoted from her extensive reading. Inspired by the Spirit, her words were powerful and persuasive. Many Quakers in Philadelphia recognized that the young woman had a genuine gift. Although not yet 30 years old, Lucretia was formally recognized in 1821 as a Quaker minister.

Although Lucretia's ideas did not yet cause the public outcry they would in later years, some people took issue with certain things she said. For example, some Friends once visited at her house and, after sitting in silence for some time, they asked her what she had meant when she spoke at the last Meeting. Lucretia repeated the exact quotation she had used: "Men are to be judged by their likeness to Christ, rather than their notions of Christ." She asked her visitors if that had been the offending passage. It was, but the Friends were surprised to learn that those words were not Lucretia's. They had been written by William Penn, the Quaker who founded the colony of Pennsylvania.

Despite occasional criticism, Lucretia did not shy from speaking out against unfairness, even when it was perpetrated by members of her own Quaker group, or Meeting. Sometimes the discipline applied by the Meeting, Lucretia felt, was the result of ignorance and intolerance. She protested when the Meeting chose to disown a poor woman whose daughter married a man who was not a full member. Lucretia felt such harsh punishment was ridiculous, and she feared practices like this would one day jeopardize Quakerism itself.

Lucretia and James were disturbed when the Society of Friends in Wilmington, Delaware, disowned some members who had attended a lecture on education given by Fanny Wright. The offense? Fanny Wright spoke to "promiscuous" audiences—that is, audiences consisting of both men and women. Lucretia's and James's protests over this case put both the Motts in danger of being disowned by their own Meeting. But Lucretia felt strongly that it was wrong to punish people merely for listening to new ideas.

In 1823 Lucretia had another son, whom she also named Thomas Coffin Mott. When not involved with her ministry, Lucretia was busy at home, caring for her children and running her household. The older children went to local schools until they were old enough to attend Westtown.

James was a wholesaler now, finally doing well

enough to support his growing family. He was assisted by an extremely thrifty Lucretia, who kept her hands always busy mending old pillows and sheets, turning and repairing carpets, and knitting. In 1824 the Motts moved away from the joint Coffin-Mott household and set up their own home at Sansom Street. And soon another daughter, Elizabeth, was born, in 1825.

Shortly afterward the family was struck by several tragedies. Older sister Sarah suffered a fall and died. Younger sister Mary, who had married Solomon Temple, died giving birth to her second child. Anna Coffin took in her daughter's two young children, but one died shortly afterward. After sister Martha returned home from school, she soon eloped with a Captain Peter Pelham to Florida. When Martha returned to Philadelphia to have her first baby at home, the Quaker Meeting disowned her. Then Martha learned that her husband had died during her absence.

Lucretia, always close to her family and ready to help as much as she could, was deeply affected by this series of tragic events. All these bereavements taught her not to set store by earthly pleasures, and she turned instead to a deepening spiritual life as she continued to search for the path of duty. She took her young niece, Anna Temple, into her home and cared for her and her own four children, nursing them all through a bout of the measles. Life became even busier with the birth of one more daughter, Martha, who was called "Pattie," in 1828.

During the late 1820s the issue of slavery began to weigh more and more heavily on Lucretia's and James's minds. They were particularly bothered that James's business dealt heavily in cotton, produced by slave labor. In 1818 Lucretia had witnessed slavery for the first time when visiting Virginia with a Quaker woman minister. Lucretia was shocked when told that the people she saw wearing rags and bound by shackles and chains were owned by "kindly" masters. During the 1820s, in

Philadelphia, Lucretia heard reports of escaped slaves being captured and returned to their owners. She also knew of cases where free blacks had been kidnapped and taken to the South as slaves.

James was already a member of the Pennsylvania Abolition Society, which had been founded in 1775 to end slavery in the United States. His duties for the group involved supervising a Philadelphia school for black children. Through James, Lucretia learned that although some free blacks in the city were prosperous, most were not. The children at the school, James reported, were often too hungry to concentrate on learning. Lucretia's heart went out to all in the city who were suffering, whether black or white, and she felt the institution of slavery allowed such wrongs to

In the late 1820s, Lucretia decided that the institution of slavery was a injustice she could not support. Her first action was to boycott anything produced by slave labor, which included sugar and cotton goods. Lucretia was particularly disturbed by the inhumane conditions under which field slaves worked and eventually helped convince her husband to switch from selling cotton to wool.

exist. Still, she thought, what could she, a housewife and mother, do?

At Meeting one day, Lucretia felt inspired to act. She decided to boycott all products produced by slave labor. This would be a hardship, she knew, but as biographer Margaret Hope Bacon described, Lucretia believed it was her duty: "No more sugar, no more cotton, no more writing paper with rag content, no more molasses. . . . Moreover, what was she to do with a husband who dealt in cotton? Never mind, it was on her alone the duty had been laid and it was she who must be faithful."

James was bothered, too, but he was reluctant to risk plunging his family into poverty again. However, in 1826 he and other Quakers formed the Free Produce Society. This group publicized the boycott of slave-labor goods. It also helped support free-produce stores—that is, stores that sold only items not made by slaves. The Motts bought their children specially made candy (produced without sugar), which unfortunately wasn't very tasty. But each piece was wrapped in paper containing a little verse such as the following:

> Take this, my friend, you need not fear to eat
> No slave hath toiled to cultivate the sweet.

In 1830 James could stand the pangs of conscience no longer, and he switched from dealing in cotton to wool. Fortunately for the Motts, his business continued to thrive. And Lucretia did more than just boycotting; in Meetings she often spoke out against the evils of slavery, despite criticism from Quaker elders who objected to nonspiritual matters being introduced in worship. But to Lucretia, antislavery was spiritual. What good were piety and religion, she felt, if they did not inspire people to live moral lives? And part of living a moral life was to fight against evil and injustice.

To Lucretia Mott, as to no other reformer of the 19th century, the antislavery effort was connected with every other reform movement. She was against war and violence, against slavery, against the root causes of poverty, and she was for the right of all people to be treated with respect. To her, all of these causes were bound closely to the duty she felt was hers: to leave the world a better place than she had found it.

The abolitionist minister Elias Hicks advocated a return to simpler elements of Quakerism, an attitude opposed by most members of Philadelphia Meetings. In 1827 the Society of Friends divided into separate groups: Hicksite Quakers and Orthodox Quakers. Lucretia found herself torn between the two, although she favored the Hicksites' philosophy.

3

"WHY SHOULD WE BE COWARDS?"

During the late 1820s, while Lucretia was preaching, boycotting slave-made products, and caring for her growing family, the Society of Friends was undergoing a serious schism (a division between differing factions). The controversy centered around a Quaker minister and abolitionist named Elias Hicks. Lucretia had heard Hicks speak when she was still in school at Nine Partners, and she felt he was a good man. Hicks advocated a return to simple, traditional Quakerism; in his view, Quakers—particularly the prominent city-dwelling Friends—were paying too much attention to "outward" Christianity—that is, to the events of Christ's life such as Christmas and the Last Supper—rather than to the Inner Light.

Some Quakers, notably many in Philadelphia, objected to Hicks's ideas. They felt he was essentially denying that Christ was divine. These Quakers, with the support of the London Society of Friends, sought to restrict Hicks's speaking at Meetings. Other Quakers, who did not necessarily agree with Hicks's ideas, still believed he had a right to speak as the Spirit moved him. Hicks refused to stop speaking. In 1827 these disagreements over Hicks led to a serious rift in the Philadelphia Friends. Hicks's supporters, called "Hicksites," formed their own Meetings and refused to attend the "Orthodox" Meetings.

Although both Motts were opposed to the bickering and divisions, James Mott strongly agreed with Elias Hicks's views. Lucretia's sister Eliza, her mother, and James's mother remained in the Orthodox group. Lucretia must have been reluctant to increase the divisions in her own family, and at first she did not side openly with the Hicksites. Instead she treaded a fine line between the two groups when she was chosen to be clerk of the Philadelphia Women's Yearly Meeting.

In 1830, her first year as clerk, Lucretia was required to sign a letter to the London Society of Friends that repudiated Hicks's teachings. Quakers did not vote; it was the clerk's task to gather the "sense of the Meeting"—in other words, to go along with the general consensus. Lucretia spoke against the letter in Meeting and made some changes in its language; for example, she replaced the word "brotherly" with "friendly" and changed the word "brethren" to read "brethren and sisters." The original letter, however, was accepted by the Philadelphia Quakers and her changes were rejected. Lucretia's willingness to challenge the Orthodox Quakers made the elders keep an eye on her behavior. Still, her balancing act continued to be successful for several years. Despite the "sharp eyes" watching her, Lucretia remained influential enough within the Meeting to be clerk year after year throughout the 1830s.

While she continued to speak in Philadelphia area Meetings, Lucretia also traveled more and more frequently to speak in other Quaker communities. Often, because James's work required him to stay near Philadelphia, she undertook such journeys without a chaperon—which at that time was almost unheard-of behavior for a woman. This habit of traveling alone contributed to her image among Philadelphia Quakers as being somewhat odd. One trip took Lucretia to the home of her sister Martha, who had remarried and

THE LIBERATOR.

VOL. I.] WILLIAM LLOYD GARRISON AND ISAAC KNAPP, PUBLISHERS. [NO. 33.

BOSTON, MASSACHUSETTS.] OUR COUNTRY IS THE WORLD—OUR COUNTRYMEN ARE MANKIND. [SATURDAY, AUGUST 13, 1831.

At the age of 26, William Lloyd Garrison began publishing an antislavery newspaper, the Liberator, *and soon afterward formed the first society that called for the immediate abolition of slavery. The famous abolitionist was a frequent visitor to the Motts' home on Sansom Street.*

settled with her husband, David Wright, in Aurora, New York. During the next two years Lucretia traveled within Pennsylvania and New Jersey, and throughout the Delaware River Valley. The following year she traveled through upstate New York and then visited family members in Nantucket, Massachusetts. Here she found, to her relief, that despite the divisions between Hicksites and Orthodox Quakers, her relatives remained friendly toward her.

In 1830 Lucretia's oldest daughter Anna turned 18 years old. She married Edward Hopper, a young lawyer and the son of a famous Philadelphia abolitionist printer, Isaac Hopper.

That same year the Motts welcomed another abolitionist into their home, a young man named William Lloyd Garrison. Abolitionists knew that the Motts' home was always open to them. Garrison's visit was the start of a lifelong friendship between the Motts and him. And it also marked the beginning of Lucretia's more radical activism against slavery. Over the years Lucretia had tried to keep her more extreme feelings well hidden, but though they were hidden they did not diminish. If anything, they became even more radical.

At the time of his visit to the Motts' home, Garrison had recently been released from jail. He had been imprisoned for libel when an antislavery editorial he had written offended a prominent Southern slave trader. Garrison, however, was undeterred by his time spent in jail. In his visit with the Motts, he convinced them that the solution to abolishing slavery was not what they favored—colonization (a plan to return freed slaves to Africa). His beliefs were quite different.

In fact, Garrison was perhaps the most radical of all abolitionists: he was against gradual abolition and also against the idea of buying slaves from their masters in order to free them. Instead he favored immediate and unequivocal abolition; he opposed any scheme for emancipation (freeing of slaves) that acknowledged that

slaveholders had any right to own slaves in the first place. In 1831 Garrison had published the first issue of his newspaper, the *Liberator*, in which he thundered: "I am in earnest, I will not equivocate, I will not excuse, I will not retreat a single inch, and I will be heard."

In 1833 Great Britain abolished the slave trade, although not slavery itself, in its colonies in the West Indies. At about the same time, to capitalize on this success, Garrison helped form the American Anti-Slavery Society, and organized a national antislavery convention in Philadelphia. Lucretia opened her home to many delegates, taking on a great deal of extra housekeeping, as well as helping Garrison with the organization of the convention.

The cotton gin, invented by Eli Whitney in 1793, sped up the time-consuming process of separating cotton fiber from its seeds. The device enabled plantation owners to significantly increase cotton production, making them consider slavery, with its cheap labor, essential to their Southern way of life.

Through antislavery news-papers, books, and leaflets, abolitionists tried to educate the rest of the nation about the evils of slavery. In her home Lucretia Mott displayed pamphlets that reflected the impact of slavery on women as well as men.

Even this early in the radical abolition movement, Lucretia was notable among her fellow reformers for her insistence on including women. On the antislavery pamphlets displayed in her home, for example, the popular symbol of a slave asking, "Am I not a Man and a Brother?" was replaced by a female slave asking, "Am I not a Woman and a Sister?" Despite her insistence on remembering the women, however, Lucretia did not expect to participate fully in the national antislavery convention. None of the other women attendees did either.

However, at the convention, when no one mentioned what Lucretia saw as an error in the convention's Declaration of Sentiments, she rose to speak amidst surprised murmurs. Her comments were well received. When someone announced to the participants that a few abolitionists had already refused to sign the convention document, apparently fearing for their reputations, Lucretia spoke again: "If our principles are right, why should we be cowards? Why should we wait for those who never had the courage to maintain the inalienable rights of the slave?" And again, when a male speaker advised caution against signing, Lucretia spoke up. "James, put down thy name," she called out, and James Mott was the first to sign the document. The Motts' unhesitating support swayed others who were wavering.

Lucretia's willingness to speak, her intelligence, and her fortitude impressed one young man attending the convention—J. Miller McKim. He confessed to her that the wealth of new ideas he encountered among the abolitionists overwhelmed him, conflicting as they did with his studies to be a Presbyterian minister. Lucretia took him under her wing, loaning books, introducing him to her Quaker Meeting, and generally encouraging him to learn more. McKim himself was strongly impressed by the Motts and by Lucretia in particular. Lucretia and McKim's friendship provided both with an outlet for intellectual debate on almost any subject. Although they often disagreed, the two remained life-long friends and correspondents.

Immediately after Garrison's convention ended, Lucretia began organizing the Philadelphia Female Anti-Slavery Society, the first women's abolitionist group. Lucretia herself, however, was unfamiliar with how to run meetings, and she asked two men to help her. After the first meeting, though, the Society's members felt better able to conduct their activities without male assistance.

Both black and white women were members of the Female Anti-Slavery Society. At the time, this "mix-ing" of races horrified many respectable people, and it angered the not-so-respectable, too. Lucretia and the other women stood their ground and refused to segregate their meetings or their activities. The Female Anti-Slavery Society made it a practice to protest not only slavery but also any prejudice and injustice based on race. Lucretia herself invited her black friends to her house and preached in black churches. The Society was notable for its attention to and involvement in the black community in Philadelphia and elsewhere.

The female reform societies were the real beginning of the women's rights movement. Women made up a large proportion of antislavery activists and were the majority in the temperance movement, which sought to make alcohol illegal. Through their work in antislavery and temperance societies, women learned they were capable of leadership and organization, and they

developed otherwise unused talents for public speaking, writing political tracts, and other activities thought
unsuitable for women.

Lucretia herself, because of her firm convictions and
her willingness to act on them in the face of opposition,
and also because of her self-confidence and experience
from her years of preaching, was in the forefront of both
the abolition and women's rights movements. She
became a role model for countless other women—and
for men as well. Even Lucretia's opponents admired her
talents. Many years later, abolitionist Wendell Phillips
would describe how Lucretia typically responded to one
of his criticisms: "She put, as she well knows how, the
silken snapper on her whiplash, and proceeded to give
me the gentlest and yet most cutting rebuke. 'Twas . . .
beautifully done, so that the victim himself could enjoy
the artistic perfection of his punishment."

The radical abolitionists' activities and outspoken-
ness provoked a backlash. Violence erupted in New
York City and elsewhere as mobs opposed antislavery
meetings and conventions. Southerners in particular
feared that the abolitionists would provoke a slave
rebellion. But many Northerners, too, were opposed to
abolition. The tendency of abolitionists to support
other reforms offended many who preferred things to
remain as they were. Others believed slavery would end
on its own—somehow, someday—and so there was no
point in stirring up trouble over it.

Sometimes the fiery rhetoric of abolitionists resulted
in violence. A riot in Philadelphia in 1834 resulted in
great damage to the homes and churches of the city's
black community. The police, who arrived late, hardly
did anything to restrain the mob. Newspapers pro-
claimed that the blacks themselves had incited the riot.

Most Quakers, whether Hicksite or Orthodox,
became alarmed and feared the radicalism of the abolition movement. They advocated the formation of separate, Quaker antislavery societies. They also opposed

Harriet Martineau (1802–76) was an English writer and social reformer. When she visited the United States in 1834, she became an abolitionist and took part in antislavery activities at the Motts' Philadelphia home.

the annual fair held by the Female Anti-Slavery Society, which raised thousands of dollars, arguing that it was frivolous and conflicted with Quaker values of having a plain and simple lifestyle. Most ominously, the Quaker elders sought to restrict preaching against slavery.

Instead of silencing Lucretia Mott on the topic of slavery, the Quaker elders' actions only made Lucretia question the convictions of those elders—and by extension, Quakerism itself. In the fall of 1834, Lucretia wrote to a friend, "I can never willingly submit. William Penn said he hated obedience upon authority without conviction." If her obedience to her Inner Light led her to activities that some Quakers found objectionable, Lucretia thought, so be it. Indeed, she was criticized by some Philadelphia Quakers, as well as by those in other cities and towns. Yet she felt she had no choice but to speak out.

The endless criticism, however, resulted in health problems for Lucretia. She began to suffer from dyspepsia (stomach pain) that was so severe she was sometimes bent double with pain. Through the years Lucretia tried a number of diets to alleviate the discomfort, but she knew that its root cause was the stress of her reform activity—and she had no intention of ceasing her work. When a doctor told her she should take some time off from her abolition efforts, she responded that she would gladly do so if the doctor's wife would take her place.

Lucretia continued to welcome many houseguests, some of whom were famous figures: William Lloyd Garrison was a frequent visitor, as was former president John Quincy Adams. Other guests included friends such as Miller McKim, British writer and abolitionist Harriet Martineau, and renowned phrenologist George Combe (phrenology is the study of the human skull in the belief that its shape corresponds to a person's intelligence and personality).

In 1836 Lucretia's daughter Maria married a notable local merchant and abolitionist, Edward Davis. With the new addition to the family and their endless stream of visitors, the Motts decided to move in 1837 to a larger house on North Ninth Street. The larger house enabled the Motts to welcome even more guests. Although it was a time when many believed that if a woman had interests outside of her family, the family itself would suffer, Lucretia's ability to keep up with the housework and make the Mott home a welcoming place for all made her almost an icon among reformers.

The Motts did well financially, but they were not rich. To afford to welcome so many guests, Lucretia was strict with her spending and thrifty in her housekeeping. She was always able, no matter what their income, to give a great deal to charity. To do so, though, she denied herself and her family some plea-sures. She was sometimes lovingly teased by her family and friends for her economical habits, but she persisted throughout her life—even when such economy was not strictly necessary. No expenditure was too small for her to record in her small account book. She was noto-rious among family and friends for using small scraps of paper to write her letters. The recipient sometimes needed to solve a jigsaw puzzle before he or she could read the letter.

One humorous story was passed down through the McKim family. In the middle of a conversation with Sarah McKim, the story goes, Lucretia saw a feather floating in the air. As biographer Margaret Hope Bacon describes the incident: "Without pause in her conversation, [Lucretia] captured the piece of down, took scissors, needles and thread from a reticule at her waist, unstitched a seam in a cushion on which she was seated, tucked the feather in and repaired it before [Sarah] McKim's fascinated eyes."

But Lucretia's housework was not all that kept her busy. With an associate, Maria Chapman, the leader of Boston's Female Anti-Slavery Society, Lucretia orga-nized the first Anti-Slavery Convention of American Women. It was held in New York in 1837, the same year the Motts moved to their new, bigger house. Lucretia and her daughter Anna Mott Hopper attended this convention together. The meeting marked the start of more turmoil—this time within the abolition move-ment itself.

Lucretia Mott campaigned for the abolition of slavery at a time when society did not think it proper for women to speak in public. In the 1830s, only Quakers recognized women as ministers who could preach before Meetings. Controversy over the proper role of women in antislavery efforts soon split the abolitionist movement.

4

PROMISCUOUS AUDIENCES

I n 1835 Angelina Grimké, the abolitionist daughter of a South Carolina slaveholder, had attended a lecture given at a Philadelphia Female Anti-Slavery Society meeting. She was so impressed that she joined the Society soon afterward. Then she wrote a letter to William Lloyd Garrison expressing her support of his activities. Garrison published the letter, launching Angelina into the national spotlight. She agreed to speak publicly against slavery.

At first Angelina Grimké addressed only women. She became so popular, however, that men began attending her lectures. Hearing Angelina criticized for addressing "promiscuous" audiences, her sister Sarah, not as strident an abolitionist, decided to accompany Angelina to the 1837 Anti-Slavery Convention of American Women in New York to defend the Grimké name. After the convention, both Grimké sisters lectured on a tour of New England. Lucretia's Philadelphia Female Anti-Slavery Society sent a note of support.

The Grimkés often spoke in churches, but when a lecture in Lynn, Massachusetts, was declared open to all, and not just women, many clergymen protested. As a result, the Grimkés were refused the use of some church buildings. From then on many

New Englanders would protest the Grimkés' arrivals in their towns. The two sisters could not rent halls in which to speak, and sometimes a mob would gather and throw stones and rotten tomatoes at them.

The issue of addressing "promiscuous" audiences split the abolition movement in two. Not all abolitionists shared Lucretia's belief that the fight for the freedom of black Americans was related to the fight for the rights of women, whether black or white. Some men— and women—believed that women should speak publicly only to other women, or not speak publicly at all. Others insisted that women had not only a right to speak but also a moral duty. While many did support women's rights, they believed that it was a separate issue that should not be permitted to interfere with the abolitionist cause.

Lucretia herself supported the Grimkés' efforts and hoped their struggle would help eliminate what she called "the low estimate of woman's labors." Still, Lucretia was too busy with her own abolitionist efforts to do much more about women's rights than follow the Grimkés' progress.

In 1838 the second Anti-Slavery Convention of American Women was to be held in the newly completed Pennsylvania Hall in Philadelphia, a building for which James and Lucretia Mott had worked for years to raise money. Opposition to the convention was bitter and dangerous. Already strained by the financial panic of 1837, the working-class people of Philadelphia strongly opposed the concept of full equality of whites and "coloreds."

The week of the convention, Angelina Grimké married the abolitionist minister Theodore Weld, and both whites and blacks attended the wedding. This "mixing" was merely a prelude, the opponents of abolition thought, to racially mixed marriages. Watching white and black women going in and out of Pennsylvania Hall during the Anti-Slavery Convention further enraged

Angelina Emily Grimké (1792–1873), was a Southern slaveholder's daughter who became a devoted abolitionist. She traveled throughout the North, lecturing against the institution of slavery, and was severely criticized for speaking before "promiscuous" audiences— gatherings that included both men and women.

these abolition opponents.

By the second night, while convention delegates disagreed over the issue of whether women should speak before "promiscuous" audiences, the mob surrounding the hall swelled to 17,000. The mayor of Philadelphia, to whom the convention's delegates appealed for protection, did nothing but ask for the key to the hall. That night the mob set fire to the new building; it burned to the ground. The angry throng searched for new targets the next day. Lucretia, James, and the many guests and family members waited patiently at the Motts' house, preparing for the worst. But as the mob entered a nearby street, a friend of theirs shouted, "On

An angry crowd could not tolerate the "racial mixing" of the 3,000 black and white women attending the 1838 Anti-Slavery Convention of American Women, held in Philadelphia. Throwing rocks and shouting angrily, a mob stormed Pennsylvania Hall, but the convention participants continued on with their speeches. Later the mob returned to set the newly built hall on fire, burning it to the ground.

to the Motts!" and pointed in the wrong direction.

Although the Motts' house escaped harm, a church and an orphanage for black children were burned. The final session of the convention was held in a schoolhouse, where the women delegates agreed not to let violence stop them from continuing social relations with black friends. Instead, they resolved to expand them.

In response to the violence at Pennsylvania Hall, William Lloyd Garrison helped form the New England Non-Resistance Society in 1838. Despite the language of violence used by Garrison and other radical abolitionists, Garrison himself was a strong pacifist who practiced "nonresistant" politics. He did not believe in voting, holding office, serving on juries, or performing any other civic duty for a proslavery government. When the new Non-Resistance Society announced its extreme views, the declaration was met with an overwhelmingly negative response—even from some Quakers.

Lucretia held similarly radical views. Each reform society and group she supported was ultimately based on defending the overall causes of human rights and justice.

At the Non-Resistance Society's meeting in 1839, a resolution was introduced calling for peace not only in civic life but also in family life—that is, children in particular should not be punished. Lucretia believed that parents who spank or strike their children "overlook the fact that a child, like all other human beings, has inalienable rights. It is the master that is not prepared for emancipation and it is the parent who is not prepared to give up punishment." Even in our day, many who still believe the old saying "spare the rod, spoil the child" may consider Lucretia's view as too radical.

Lucretia's stand on the issue of nonresistance was strongly criticized by Quakers who felt she was more devoted to "worldly" issues and various societies than to religion. A prominent Quaker of New York named George White, who was an adamant opponent of the abolitionists, targeted Lucretia in particular. White was influential enough that Lucretia felt in danger of being disowned. Still, her faith in her Inner Light was such that she continued to travel and preach on abolition and nonresistance.

On one of these trips in Delaware, an angry mob attacked Lucretia's friend and relative by marriage, Daniel Neall, who was taken from their host's home. Lucretia asked that the enraged men take her instead, but they refused. "I ask no courtesy at your hands on account of my sex," Lucretia insisted. When they took Neall away, Lucretia followed, arguing with them the whole way, with no fear for her own safety. Embarrassed by her vociferous presence, the men did smear some tar on Daniel's coat and tack on a few feathers. But they let him go, otherwise unharmed. The incident became a highly touted example of successful Christian nonresistance.

In 1839 abolitionist Abby Kelley, who had spoken at the Anti-Slavery Convention at Pennsylvania Hall,

At the World Anti-Slavery Convention held in 1840, Lucretia Mott met Elizabeth Cady Stanton, who was accompanying her delegate husband Henry Stanton. Because of their treatment at the meeting, Lucretia and Elizabeth decided that the issue of women's rights in society needed to be addressed as well.

wrote to Lucretia urging that the Female Anti-Slavery Society no longer operate separately from its all-male counterpart. While Mott agreed that Kelley's proposal was logical, she felt there was nothing wrong with continuing female-only meetings, which had already helped "in bringing our sex forward, exercising their talents, and preparing them for united action with men, as soon as we can convince them that this is both our right and our duty." Lucretia did, however, invite Abby Kelley to attend the next convention and discuss the matter further.

Many of the New England abolitionists, however, including Kelley, did not attend the 1839 Anti-Slavery Convention of American Women. The abolition movement in New England was bitterly divided over the issue of how women should be involved in the abolitionist movement. Then, too, Lucretia faced many struggles just to organize the convention. Few places were willing to house the controversial group ("to the great shame of Philadelphia," Lucretia acidly remarked), particularly after the previous year's violence. Eventually, the convention was held in a stable belonging to the Pennsylvania Riding School.

Finally, the all-male American Anti-Slavery Society voted to allow women, but the men remained divided over whether to allow women to serve on committees. Amidst the factionalism, Lucretia struggled to be the peacemaker between disputing reformers, many of whom were her friends. She urged the quarreling factions to unite in public and not air their disagreements, just as she urged all parties to be at peace with one another.

But when Lucretia herself was appointed to a committee, the entire American Anti-Slavery Society split into two factions: the "Old Organization," which supported women's full involvement, and the "New Organization," which opposed it. Notable abolitionists such as John Greenleaf Whittier, Abby Kelley, and Theodore Weld chose sides, and Lucretia, friendly with all and caught in the middle, struggled in vain to make peace. Her severe dyspepsia flared up again under the strain.

During this tense time, Lucretia and James Mott were chosen to be the delegates from Pennsylvania to the 1840 World Anti-Slavery Convention in London, England. At first the Motts were unsure they could afford the trip; James's business had had some unfortunate downturns. But a sea voyage would certainly aid Lucretia's poor health, and friends sent money to ensure the Motts could attend. Even the Quaker Meeting to which the Motts belonged extended its approval.

British abolitionists had not yet suffered a schism over "the woman question" as had their American counterparts. Women in the British abolition movement were content to work in separate societies. The London convention's leaders were not prepared to admit women as delegates, no matter how experienced, talented, or prominent the individual women. Lucretia and the other women delegates, including Mary Grew, Sarah Pugh, Elizabeth Neall, and Abby Kimber (all from Pennsylvania), as well as some women from New England, refused to withdraw their credentials and insisted on admittance.

Antislavery activists in Great Britain were mostly opposed to women's inclusion in "men's work." Several of those who opposed women's full participation in the convention were concerned about Lucretia in particular. London Quakers had heard that Lucretia was a heretic, because of her support of Elias Hicks. Some even feared to welcome Lucretia into their homes, because she might influence their children to take up her "heresies."

The debate over the inclusion of women took up the entire first day of the convention. A British delegate argued that the meeting could hardly be called a World Convention if half the world were excluded. Wendell Phillips led the strenuous debate to admit women; his own wife was a delegate. Henry Stanton, too, a member of the "New Organization," nevertheless argued for women's inclusion—possibly because his new wife, Elizabeth Cady Stanton, insisted upon it.

Elizabeth Stanton was present at the convention, but not as a delegate. She and Lucretia struck up a devoted friendship during their time in London. Dismayed by the exclusion of women from the convention, as well as by other social injustices, the two agreed to organize a women's rights convention in America as soon as they could manage it.

In the end, the women, although not allowed to

serve as delegates, were welcome to sit in on the meetings and listen from a gallery behind a screen. William
Lloyd Garrison, who arrived late, refused to take part in
the convention because of the exclusion of women. He
chose to sit behind the screen as well. Daniel O'Connell, a "great Irish orator," was honored to go behind
the screen to meet Lucretia; she was polite but blunt
with him. She wrote a friend that O'Connell offered
"flattering compliments which we could not receive in
place of rights denied."

Lucretia did not feel called to speak at the convention, or she very likely would have, despite the ban. In
London she contended not only with overt sexism but
also with the charge of "heresy." Nevertheless, she

Only men could participate in the proceedings of the World Anti-Slavery Convention. Women delegates were seated in a separate gallery and not allowed to speak. In protest, prominent abolitionist William Lloyd Garrison refused to participate in the conference, and he sat with the women for its duration.

continued to work behind the scenes to right the injustice of the women's exclusion. She preached at churches when she was invited, encouraged others to write letters of protest, and even organized a small meeting of women at the lodging house. Her presence at the convention despite the ruling served to remind people of the exclusion—but some radicals felt she compromised the ideal of women's equal rights by continuing to attend.

After the convention, James and Lucretia spent some time in London, seeing the sights. But Lucretia was more fascinated by people, and she did not find most of the tourist sites very interesting. At the London Zoo, a man viewing the brightly colored birds needled Lucretia about her drab Quaker garb. "God believed in bright colors," the man said, pointing to the birds.

"Yes," Lucretia shot back, "but immortal beings do not depend on feathers for their attractions. Moreover, if it is fitting that woman should dress in every color of the rainbow, why not man also?"

At the British Museum Lucretia and Elizabeth Cady Stanton chose to sit and talk while the others in their group explored the massive, world-renowned collections. When the group returned hours later, they found the two women sitting in the same place, deep in animated discussion.

In July the Motts traveled to the cities of Birmingham and Manchester, England, as well as to the countries of Ireland and Scotland. Lucretia was invited to preach in a Unitarian church in Scotland, where for the first time she spoke extensively about women's rights. She urged women to "brush away the silken fetters that have bound them" and to "fit themselves to assume their proper position in being the natural companions, the friends, the instructors of the race."

At the summer's end the Motts returned home, with Lucretia's health fully restored, despite the conflicts in the British Isles. One biographer reasons that Lucretia's health improved because her critics were strangers: "Lucretia had therefore felt justified in fighting back rather than holding herself and her anger in check." The trip, despite the exclusion of women from the convention, was a success.

Upon her return, Lucretia was hailed as the leading woman reformer not only in the abolition movement, but in the newly burgeoning area of women's rights. And the trip had produced a change in Lucretia too: from now on, the already outspoken woman became even less willing to hold her tongue, or her anger, in check.

Lucretia and James Mott, both tireless reformers, were determined to leave the world a better place than they found it. Husband and wife steadfastly supported each other's causes throughout their 56-year-long marriage.

5

THE ROAD TO SENECA FALLS

ortified by the struggle in London, Lucretia was even more determined to continue her outspoken efforts to end slavery and improve the standing of women. The coming decade would witness her increasing radicalism and also her unwillingness to placate her opponents by giving ground.

Accompanied by James, Lucretia spoke in several Meetings throughout Delaware and Pennsylvania in the fall of 1840, and she even addressed three state legislatures about slavery (Pennsylvania, New Jersey, and Delaware). Opposition to her efforts and to her as an individual continued. In Smyrna, Delaware, where Lucretia and her friend Daniel Neall had faced an angry mob earlier, Lucretia spoke at a Meeting. Afterward, the Motts learned that someone—perhaps the leader of the mob—had tampered with the wheels of their carriage. Fortunately, the damage was discovered before an accident resulted. Then the town innkeeper, surrounded by yet another hostile crowd, politely made excuses as to why he could not spare a room for the Motts. They were forced to drive much further and stay at a friend's home.

In the fall of 1841 Lucretia preached at a Meeting in New York,

The Motts belonged to several abolitionist organizations, including the Pennsylvania Anti-Slavery Society. In this photograph of its executive committee Lucretia Mott and her husband James are seated at the right.

then continued on to Boston to address the New England Non-Resistance Society. Her speech at Marlboro Chapel expressed her liberal views on many topics, perhaps most radically on women's rights: "I long for the time when my sisters will rise, and occupy the sphere to which they are called by their high nature and destiny."

Back in Philadelphia, Lucretia again faced criticism from well-meaning Quaker elders who worried about her increased militancy since her return from London. The criticism was trivial in some cases; for example, a new bonnet, given to her by friends in England, was not quite plain enough for Philadelphia Quakers. Lucretia was willing to be flexible on such matters; she packed the bonnet away.

Still, despite the criticism, Lucretia was respected and influential enough to be chosen, along with another minister, to visit all the Quaker Meetings in central and western Pennsylvania. As writer Ralph Waldo Emerson later remarked about the Quakers' attitude toward Lucretia, "I do not wonder that they are too proud of her and too much in awe of her to spare her, though they suspect her faith."

It was not hard to be in awe of Lucretia. The 1841–42 wintertime journey through the back roads of Pennsylvania did not faze her or drain any of her boundless energy. In addition to attending all the Meetings, the 48-year-old woman arranged separate gatherings where she could speak against slavery without offending those Quakers who did not wish to hear about it.

George White, the New York Quaker who opposed the antislavery movement, took action against several Quaker abolitionists in 1841 and 1842. He protested to Lucretia's Meeting in Philadelphia that she should not have preached in New York without the written support of her own Meeting. In 1842 White also insisted that abolitionist Isaac Hopper be disowned by the Society of Friends. In response, Lucretia's son-in-law Edward— Isaac's son—withdrew from the Philadelphia Quaker Meeting. The Motts were saddened by this event, but they understood Edward's decision and supported him. There seemed to be no end to the painful divisions among Lucretia's family and friends.

During the 1840s, attitudes stiffened against abolitionists as the North and the South compromised to prevent the issue of slavery from splitting the country. The U.S. Congress refused to discuss petitions about slavery, hoping that avoiding the subject would keep the peace. Southern legislators outlawed the publication and distribution of antislavery literature. In the North, mobs continued to gather and riot during abolitionists' speeches and at their conventions.

In 1842 James and Lucretia took their efforts to the South itself. Lucretia spoke at a Meeting in Baltimore, Maryland, and then traveled on through Virginia, where she met with slaveholders themselves to discuss the antislavery issue. Afterward James and Lucretia returned home, convinced that Southern men and women were as open to their cause as some Northerners, who often gave lip service to the problem but refused to take any action.

In January 1843 Lucretia spoke in a Unitarian church in Washington, D.C., after she had been prevented from addressing the U.S. House of Representatives. However, many congressmen attended her speech at the church, where her words transfixed her audience. Among the rapt listeners was essayist and poet Ralph Waldo Emerson, who later wrote his wife that "it was like the rumble of an earthquake." The petite, plainly-dressed Quaker woman, as always, spoke her mind as the Spirit moved her. Her radical, liberal words seemed quite at variance with her gentle demeanor and sober appearance, but she spoke with a glow that impressed the audience whether they agreed with her or not.

After the speech, James and Lucretia went to the White House to speak with the president himself—without an invitation! President John Tyler was known for his support of states' rights, which aligned him politically with the South. He received the Motts politely, but he felt that the answer to the slavery question was colonization in Africa, not the immediate freeing of slaves. The Motts disagreed with him. Tyler questioned whether there was any alternative. Did the Motts want all the proposed freedmen living in the North?

"Yes, as many as want to come," Lucretia responded.

Tyler remained unconvinced, but he was plainly dazzled by Lucretia. "I would like to hand Mr. Calhoun over to you," he remarked, referring to John Calhoun, the Southern representative known for his debating skills.

After Lucretia's return to Philadelphia, she found her critics willing to speak more boldly than ever. In several meetings Lucretia's views were disputed, and though

American essayist Ralph Waldo Emerson (1803–1882) was impressed whenever he heard Lucretia Mott speak. He described her powerful address before an audience in Washington, D.C., as like "the rumble of an earthquake."

she sometimes preached in response, she was occasionally prevented from doing so. In 1843 Lucretia's Meeting refused its support for her preaching. She continued to travel anyway, but now she was often received coldly, ordered to sit down when she tried to speak, and sometimes turned away.

The 1840s were a tense time for Lucretia as she searched her conscience for the right path to take. She considered resigning from the Society of Friends. Even the Hicksites, she felt, were falling victim to the same intolerance that they had rebelled against in the 1820s and 1830s.

In the face of hurtful attacks, Lucretia turned to her

In an 1843 meeting with President John Tyler, Lucretia Mott demanded that the nation institute an immediate ban on slavery. Although her words were forceful, she could not convince Tyler to take any action.

large circle of supportive and admiring family and friends. Her relationship with James, always strong, continued to deepen. The couple presented a united front in public at all times. On one occasion Lucretia sharply corrected a well-known minister in a public meeting, and the man turned to James Mott for his opinion. "If she thinks thee wrong, thee had better think it over again," James responded. Whatever others might say, Lucretia could always count on James's firm and unwavering support.

Lucretia kept in contact, too, with Elizabeth Cady Stanton, who was busy raising her children practically alone, since Henry Stanton traveled frequently. Elizabeth took strength from Lucretia's encouragement. Stanton wrote, "I found in this new friend a woman emancipated from all faith in man-made creeds, from all fear of his denunciations."

Tragedy struck the Mott family again in early 1844, when both Lucretia and her mother fell ill with a form of influenza. Anna Coffin died at the end of March. Lucretia, deeply grief stricken, barely had time to recover from her own bout with the illness when she came down with encephalitis (an inflammation of the brain). Lucretia's family and friends feared she might not live. Her sister Martha Wright came from New York to nurse her, and after a month or so Lucretia finally recovered.

Another minor crisis followed. Apparently, Lucretia's son, Thomas, and Martha's daughter Marianne had been in love for some time. Though they tried to repress their feelings—Marianne was actually already engaged to a prominent Quaker—the two young people decided to marry despite being first cousins. "How little Marianne knew us to suppose we should oppose them if their hearts were so deeply interested," Lucretia wrote to Martha. Although Thomas was disowned by his Meeting for the marriage, both his parents supported his decision.

Lucretia recovered from her illnesses over the summer and bounced back into energetic action, beginning with a visit to Martha in New York. During this trip Lucretia also visited Community Farm, an experimental commune run by abolitionists and other reformers.

In the fall, back in Philadelphia, the activist formed a new organization—the Association for the Relief of Poor Women (later called the Northern Association). This group established a place where poor women could work together sewing items ordered by wealthy customers. At Lucretia's insistence and under her leadership, both black and white women were welcome.

World events in 1846 had a profound effect on the Mott family. The United States and Britain were close to armed conflict over rights to the Oregon Territory.

In England, peace-minded groups, including Quakers, wrote to their counterparts in the United States urging a joint action to avert war. Members of Lucretia's group had written a response to the women of Exeter, England, but Lucretia believed the letter was "overly sentimental." She called for a new reply, "which it is intended shall better assert the dignity and be more fitting the intelligence of the women of the present day."

The United States and Great Britain reached a compromise just before the Meeting was held, but Lucretia Mott read the newly composed letter before the group anyway. It urged women to take increasing responsibility in peacemaking efforts. It also reminded the British people of the idea of brotherhood of race.

Also during this time, a great famine in Ireland caused by potato blight had resulted in an influx of poor Irish to American cities. Many of these new immigrants were being met with widespread prejudice. In response, James Mott raised funds for relief to be sent to Ireland, and Lucretia placed many newly arrived Irish as servants in her own and relatives' homes. She insisted on paying the servants high wages, regardless of whether they were good at their jobs. James and Lucretia also continued their practice of bringing groceries to poor families every Sunday.

Because of her many interests, Lucretia was thought "flighty" by some, particularly by a few Quaker elders. But she did not flit from one reform to another; she kept working for her many causes even as she added more to the list. In addition to her frequent travels, her ministry, and her caring for her large extended family, she regularly delivered baskets to the poor, found jobs for her seamstresses, distributed antislavery literature to the newspapers, and visited her sister and her cousins, not to mention her own daughters and grandchildren.

In 1846 Lucretia and James moved their household to the building next door, which gave their daughter Maria and her family more living space. Although the

As this political cartoon illustrates, the "Oregon Question" (a disagreement over the territory's boundary line) brought England and America close to armed conflict in 1846. Lucretia Mott supported peacemaking efforts and was relieved when a subsequent treaty established Oregon's northern boundary at the 49th parallel.

two families were next-door neighbors, the house was altered so that it could also function as a double-large home when Lucretia's house contained too many visitors.

That same year, during one of Martha's visits to Philadelphia, the two sisters decided to attend a Unitarian church convention in the city. At the invitation of the abolitionist minister of the church, Lucretia spoke before the gathering. When her speech was published in newspapers, which claimed erroneously that Lucretia had spoken as an official representative of the Society of Friends, public criticism erupted. Yet again Lucretia was accused of heresy, and shortly afterward George White again preached against her in Philadelphia.

Lucretia remained outspoken and grew ever more

The Great Hunger in Ireland (1845–47), caused by the potato blight, killed hundreds of thousands. Starving peasants were evicted to workhouses (poorhouses), such as the one shown here, while others emigrated to America. Lucretia Mott helped provide jobs and housing for many needy Irish who fled to Philadelphia.

radical. Abby Kelley, who saw Lucretia speak in Worcester, Massachusetts, in July 1847, wrote to her husband that Lucretia now espoused many causes, "from laying aside the whip stick in families to that of thorough nonresistance, temperance, antislavery, woman's rights, moral reform. I thought her decidedly more radical than when I saw her last."

Later in 1847 Lucretia and James traveled to Ohio and Indiana to attend Quaker Yearly Meetings. In Indiana they found a frosty welcome: some Hicksite elders met the Motts and asked them not to attend, or at any rate to please keep quiet during the Meeting sessions. Instead of being invited to stay with local

Quakers, as was the custom, the couple had to stay in a boardinghouse. They attended Meetings anyway, but whenever Lucretia spoke, she was not only ill received but rebuked.

This tension resulted in poor health for Lucretia, so she sought help from a local physician. Even here she was spurned, when the Quaker physician refused to see her, saying, "I am so deeply afflicted by thy rebellious spirit, that I do not feel I can prescribe for thee." Despite the pain, Lucretia insisted on attending the remainder of the sessions, hoping that by her presence she would remind the Indiana Friends of their duty to the principles of Quakerism.

After the cold reception Lucretia suffered in Indiana, she no longer held back. She finally reasoned that since her fellow Quakers were calling her a heretic, they might as well hear some radical thoughts. In early 1848 the Motts joined William Lloyd Garrison's new cause, and agreed to speak at the Anti-Sabbath Convention in Boston.

According to early Quaker principles, which the Motts strongly advocated, no day of the week is more holy than any other day. In the 1840s, the Sabbath was strictly observed in the United States, and the Motts considered the restrictions excessive. For years, Lucretia had often been forced to put her ever-present sewing away on Sundays (which Quakers called First-Days) lest she shock anyone who came to call. The compulsory observance of the Sabbath made life needlessly difficult for workers who, on their one day off, were not allowed to pursue any kind of recreational activity. Abolitionists had been arrested for handing out antislavery literature on the Sabbath.

Lucretia noted the hypocrisy of people who restricted any and all activities on Sunday but also supported slavery: "It is regarded a greater crime to do an innocent thing on the first day of the week [Sunday]—to use the needle for instance—than to put a human being on the auction block on the second day [Monday]."

Lucretia's involvement with a very controversial cause extended her reputation for heresy across the entire United States. Shortly after speaking at the Anti-Sabbath Convention, Lucretia attended the American Anti-Slavery Society annual meeting in New York. Here she gave an even more radical speech, in which she said that modern abolitionists—those rabble-rousers—represented "the Jesus of the present age on the Mount Zion of Freedom." Likening fiery abolitionists to Christ himself did not endear her to her critics.

But Lucretia continued. A few months later she addressed a group of medical students in Philadelphia. The city at that time was the center of medical training in the United States. Many students were Southerners, and several dozen walked out when Lucretia mentioned slavery. Then, too, she also supported the new and outrageous idea of training women to be doctors.

Lucretia's increasing radicalism during the 1840s was reflected in some of her outward practices: she stopped kneeling to pray when in public, and she stopped removing her bonnet when she spoke. When she wrote letters to friends, she addressed the envelopes to the women themselves, rather than to their husbands, as was the accepted practice.

Even in the face of her increasing disputes with the Society of Friends, Lucretia insisted that her actions as a leading reformer were solidly in line with the spirit of Christianity in general and Quakerism in particular. She believed that Christians must act on their beliefs, instead of waiting quietly until moved by the Spirit. This belief in acting on one's principles was not heresy, Lucretia insisted, "The great heresy is to await in a kind of indifference for the Light to come to us."

In June 1848 James and Lucretia Mott traveled to New York State, where they visited the Cattaraugus reservation for Seneca Indians and several settlements founded by escaped slaves. Afterward the Motts stayed with Lucretia's sister Martha Wright at her home in Auburn. Lucretia was eager to visit Elizabeth Cady Stanton, who had recently moved from Boston to the nearby town of Seneca Falls.

A mutual Quaker friend in Seneca Falls, Jane Hunt, invited several women—Lucretia Mott, Martha Wright, Elizabeth Cady Stanton, and Mary Ann McClintock—to a tea party. At the gathering, Elizabeth, who had had a rough year, poured out her complaints, many of which she had held since childhood, about the status of women. She said later that "I stirred myself, as well as the rest of the party to do and dare anything." By evening, the women had written a short advertisement to be published in the *Seneca County Courier* the next day, July 14, 1848:

> SENECA FALLS CONVENTION
> Woman's rights Convention—a Convention to discuss the social, civil, and religious conditions and rights of woman, will be held in the Wesleyan Chapel at Seneca Falls, N.Y. on Wednesday and Thursday, the 19th and 20th of July current; commencing at 10 o'clock A.M. During the first day the meeting will be exclusively for women, who are earnestly invited to attend. The Public generally are invited to be present on the second day when Lucretia Mott, of Philadelphia, and other ladies and gentlemen will address the convention.

The tea party had started a movement that would rock the world.

Two women with a vision were Elizabeth Cady Stanton (left) and Lucretia Mott. Eight years after they met at the World Anti-Slavery Convention and first discussed the idea, the two helped organize a women's rights meeting in Seneca Falls, New York. At that conference, the question of woman suffrage, or the right to vote, was raised publicly for the first time.

6

"THE ACTIVE BUSINESS OF LIFE"

ow that a women's rights convention was called, what would the women say? They held another tea party—a meeting to discuss declarations, resolutions, and topics for speeches. The magnitude of their task suddenly seemed overwhelming; none of the temperance and antislavery pamphlets they searched through was radical enough to be used as a model. The pamphlets were all "too tame and pacific for the likes of a rebellion such as the world had never seen," Elizabeth Cady Stanton said.

But then Stanton came up with the idea of rewriting the Declaration of Independence to reflect the women's ideas and goals. Instead of listing the unfair tyrannous actions of King George against the colonies, this declaration listed the unfair actions of men against women:

> We hold these truths to be self-evident: that all men and women are created equal. . . .
> The history of mankind is a history of repeated injuries and usurpations on the part of man toward woman, having in direct object the establishment of an absolute tyranny over her. To prove this, let facts be submitted to a candid world. . . .

In his speech at the Seneca Falls convention, former slave and renowned speaker Frederick Douglass persuaded reluctant participants to approve the resolution calling for a woman's right to vote.

He has never permitted her to exercise her inalienable right to the elective franchise. . . .

He has compelled her to submit to laws, in the formation of which she had no voice. . . .

He has made her, if married, in the eyes of the law, civilly dead.

It was the first time anyone suggested that women had a right to vote. (The women were always careful to note the difference between asking to be allowed to vote, and declaring that they had a natural right to vote that had been denied them.) It was a shocking idea, and one that many people were not ready to consider. Even Lucretia at first remarked to her friend Elizabeth, "Why Lizzie, thee will make us ridiculous!"

The women were proud of their Declaration of Sentiments, but they still had no idea how many people—if any—would attend their meeting. Still, they had waited long enough to make a start, and the convention, whatever the outcome, was now inevitable.

As Lucretia and James drove toward Seneca Falls for the first day of the convention, they found the roads choked with wagons. Soon about 300 people had filled the chapel. And although only women were supposed to attend the first day, the organizers decided to allow men to participate anyway. Uneasy about chairing a large, mixed assembly, the women asked James Mott to fill that role. James's public support was in marked contrast to Henry Stanton's—who refused to attend the convention.

The first day saw the reading, debating, and finally acceptance of the women's Declaration of Sentiments. Several resolutions were introduced, too, demanding equal status for both men and women and the repeal of laws that subjugated women. One resolution requested that women who addressed public meetings no longer be considered "indelicate" or improper, and it called for "woman's advancement in the professions." Another resolution, the most controversial, demanded "the sacred right of elective franchise"—that is, the vote. A powerful speech given by Frederick Douglass, the escaped slave who had become a leading abolitionist and orator, swayed those at the convention who were inclined to oppose this controversial item. The resolutions all passed, despite Lucretia's fear that the women would appear "ridiculous." The Seneca Falls convention is seen today as one of the most important events in the history of women's rights.

On the whole, the organizers thought, the convention had been a surprising success. But newspapers across the country had a field day criticizing the event, and they did not shy away from personal attacks on the women who organized it. Lucretia, as the most prominent among the attendees, bore the brunt of the criticism. She and the other women were called a bunch of frustrated, bitter old maids, and the meeting itself was referred to as a "hen convention" or "petticoat convention." However, the women had known before they'd started their struggle that it would be long and difficult. The expected criticism did not stop them from organizing a second convention, to be held in Rochester, New York, a few weeks later.

The second women's rights convention, though smaller, was significant in that for the first time women presided over the assembly. It was perhaps more lively than the Seneca Falls meeting, because of the presence of critics and hecklers in the audience. One man announced that if women's voices were equal to those of their husbands, the family itself would disintegrate. He also quoted Saint Paul, who instructed, "Wives, obey your husbands."

Lucretia responded that in the Quaker faith no wife vowed to obey her husband. She explained that "decisions were made by appeals not to authority but to reason." And as for Saint Paul, "Many of the opposers of Woman's Rights who bid us obey the bachelor Saint Paul, themselves reject his counsel. He advised them not to marry." Elsewhere in Saint Paul's writings, Lucretia noted, he gave instructions for women to minister and prophesy.

Another argument was made that women were intellectually inferior. Lucretia—who thought that if women indeed were inferior, it was because of their many years of limited opportunities and insufficient education—asked, "Does a man have fewer rights than another because his intellect is inferior? If not, why should a woman?"

But Lucretia, though stridently radical, was reasonable too, and she restrained those supporters who got a little carried away. When another man rose to claim that he thought women were actually superior to men in

some ways, Lucretia thanked him for the compliment but reminded him that what was needed was equality, not superiority.

Back in Philadelphia after the historic convention, Lucretia wrote letters to Elizabeth Cady Stanton, encouraging her plans to write a book about the history of women's rights. She also wanted Elizabeth and her friends to come to Philadelphia to help organize another convention. "You are so wedded to this cause, you must expect to act as pioneers in the work," she wrote to Stanton. And in a sentiment that has been echoed by American women down to the present day, Lucretia advised Elizabeth to see how far women had already come: "Look back to the days of our grandmothers and be cheered."

For Lucretia Mott, though, antislavery work took precedence. She was soon busy with preparations for

Abolitionists welcomed news of slaves successfully escaping north to freedom. The Pennsylvania Anti-Slavery Society assisted in one daring and quite unusual effort when Henry Brown was shipped as merchandise from Richmond, Virginia, to Philadelphia.

Lucretia and James Mott helped found the world's first medical school for women, the Female Medical College, shown here in its first year of operation. Now a part of Hahnemann School of Medicine, the college celebrated its 150th anniversary in the year 2000.

the Annual Anti-Slavery Fair. And she continued to devote herself to the growing abolitionist movement.

In March 1849 Lucretia's friend Miller McKim witnessed one of the most surprising and famous events of the abolitionist crusade. Henry Brown, a slave in Richmond, Virginia, decided to mail himself to freedom. He was packed into a wooden crate and shipped to the Philadelphia office of the Pennsylvania Anti-Slavery Society—which had been warned of his arrival. After a journey of 27 hours without food, sometimes resting on his head for hours, the man arrived unhurt. The box was opened in the presence of several Philadelphia abolitionists, who were moved to tears by the success. The man was thereafter known as "Box" Brown.

This happy event was overshadowed by the sudden illness and death of Lucretia's brother Thomas, at the

age of 51. She herself served as her brother's under-
taker, and to distract herself from her grief, she invited
a poor family—a mother and seven children—to stay at
her house. Caring for eight extra people kept Lucretia
busy for a time. Then in the fall of 1849 she again
invited Elizabeth Cady Stanton to Philadelphia. Stanton, however, was busy and unable to get away.

In December 1849, Lucretia gave one of her most
famous speeches, "Discourse on Woman," which was
transcribed and later published as a pamphlet. In the
speech, Lucretia first recognizes the scriptural state-
ments that appear to justify women's unequal status.
Then using her own careful reason and logic, she
shoots each interpretation down. She calls for the
"removal of obstacles" on women's path to create an
equality that is natural—not subversive: "True, nature
had made a difference in [woman's] configuration, her
physical strength, her voice—and we ask no change, we
are satisfied with nature. But how neglect and misman-
agement increased the difference!"

Lucretia goes on to declare that a woman "asks
nothing as a favor, but as a right, she wants to be
acknowledged a moral, responsible being. She is seek-
ing not to be governed by laws in the making of which
she has no voice." Lucretia recognized that many
women had learned to "hug their chains" and oppose
women's rights, but she notes that these women need
opportunities to vote, to own their own property, to be
educated, so they would appreciate their freedom.

"Let woman then go on—not asking favors, but
claiming as a right the removal of all hindrances to her
elevation in the scale of being—let her receive encouragement for the proper cultivation of her powers,
so that she may enter profitably into the active business
of life," she concludes. The speech is all the more
remarkable because Lucretia spoke extemporaneously;
she never wrote out her speeches or prepared for
them beforehand.

Although an accomplished orator, Lucretia always preferred practical, concrete action over debate. The Motts raised money to found and support the first medical school for women—the Female Medical College of Pennsylvania, which opened in late 1850. They also helped support the newly established School of Design for Women, now called the Moore College of Art. In all her other reform work Lucretia continued to address the need for change in society's attitudes towards women. Lucretia would speak out against other abolitionists and reformers when they neglected to see the connection between rights for blacks and rights for women.

Finally, Lucretia decided it was time to withdraw a bit from public life. She was a grandmother, nearing her sixties, and James had retired from business in 1851. The Motts moved to a still larger house on Arch Street, taking their ever-growing extended family along. Around the same time Thomas Mott and son-in-law Edward Davis bought some land in the hills north of Philadelphia, which included a comfortable farmhouse called Roadside. The entire family would spend vacations there together, and in 1857, James and Lucretia would sell their city home and live year-round at Roadside.

But retirement was not to be. For the rest of her life Lucretia would continue to work for a dozen causes—and second only to abolition would be women's rights. As one of Lucretia's biographers sums up the situation:

> [Lucretia] was by far the principal personage in the infant woman's rights struggle, and her gentle authority was badly needed to defend it from the attacks of its detractors as well as to restrain some of the excesses of its well-wishers. For the next thirty years she was to try, time and time again, to encourage younger women to take her place, only to be catapulted back onto center stage. There is no question that her role was crucial in the development of the movement, not only for the obvious leadership she gave,

Lucretia Mott's early role in the women's rights movement provided guidance for later activists such as Susan B. Anthony (1820–1906). But even in Anthony's lifetime, the goal of woman's suffrage would not be achieved.

but for the nurturing care . . . she provided to Elizabeth Cady Stanton, Susan B. Anthony, Lucy Stone, and a host of others.

In the early 1850s, Lucretia had despaired of holding a national women's rights convention in Philadelphia; not enough women in the city seemed interested. Nevertheless, even as overcommitted as she always was, Lucretia and her friend Mary Grew found the time to call a regional convention to be held in West Chester, Pennsylvania, in June 1852.

Buoyed by this successful convention, Lucretia agreed to attend, but not preside over, a national women's rights convention to be held in Syracuse, New York, later that year. Once she was there, however, a

Although Lucretia did not sport the new fashion called "bloomers," she did support a woman's right to wear the comfortable outfit. Named after the temperance reformer Amelia Bloomer, who first publicized the costume, bloomers gave women more freedom of movement than the heavy, long skirts of the time.

near-unanimous vote called her to chair the convention. Only her husband voted against her, out of concern for her health.

Lucretia did preside over the Syracuse meeting, which proved particularly wearing. Again and again she vacated the chairmanship to answer vociferous criticism from opponents. Attending this convention for the first time was Susan B. Anthony, who had been out of town and unable to accompany her father, Daniel, to the first two women's rights conventions in Seneca Falls and Rochester.

Despite intense opposition, the women's rights movement had gained supporters during the 1850s, as well as both positive and negative attention. One of the most notable attention-getters was a new outfit advocated by Amelia Bloomer, editor of the *Lily*, a temperance movement newspaper. The "bloomer" costume, as it came to be called, consisted of baggy trousers worn underneath a tea-length (reaching to about midcalf) skirt; the outfit did not require a corset (a tight-fitting, hooked and laced undergarment worn to produce a small waist), which was the accepted fashion of the time.

Although the bloomer costume completely covered the wearer's body, the outfit was considered vulgar. Those women who dared to wear it, however, found it very comfortable. It allowed a greater range of motion and freed them to use both hands to carry things, rather than have to lift their heavy skirts, while they walked.

Lucretia herself, although always dressed in plain Quaker gray and a shawl, defended the "bloomer women." Her 1853 speech at the Fourth National Woman's Rights Convention in Cleveland, Ohio, mentioned how she heard a woman remark that the bloomer costume was "an insult to decency." And yet, Lucretia noted, the woman speaking had been "laced so tight she could scarcely breathe, [with] clothes so long that when she went out into the dusty streets her garments formed a kind of broom to gather up the dust. This is beautiful? This is fashionable?" Nevertheless, the criticism and rude stares directed toward the bloomer wearers soon caused the fad to die out.

The passage of the Fugitive Slave Act in 1850 had forced Lucretia to focus most of her efforts on the cause of abolition. The Fugitive Slave Law required that any escaped slave found in the North must be returned to slavery. In response to the passage of the act, abolitionists worked to extend the Underground Railroad several hundred miles further into Canada and urged people to disregard the law. For radicals like the "Garrisonians," such civil disobedience was an extension of their belief

In a deadly shoot-out with abolitionist John Brown, U.S. Marines stormed the engine house he had captured at Harpers Ferry, Virginia, in hopes of inciting a slave rebellion. Although sympathetic to the cause of abolishing slavery, Lucretia disapproved of Brown's violent tactics but lent support to his wife.

in nonresistance. For others who were not as radical but were still opposed to slavery, the Fugitive Slave Law was the first law they had ever broken.

In September 1851 a violent incident occurred at a farm near the town of Christiana, in Lancaster County, Pennsylvania. A group of blacks led by the escaped slave William Parker was sheltering four runaways there. When the slave owner and his son arrived with federal marshals to reclaim the fugitives, the black men resisted. Three white neighbors, including two Quakers, arrived at the farm but refused to help the slave owner recover his "property." After the neighbors left,

Parker's band shot and killed the slave owner and wounded his son.

The three whites and 38 blacks—some of whom were not even present when the incident took place—were arrested and charged with treason. Lucretia and others came to their support; she and James raised money for their defense and ensured the defendants had warm, clean clothes before the trial began in December. The men were acquitted, but barely.

Pacifists themselves, the Motts and other non-resisters struggled with the idea that some abolitionists were willing to use violence, even in self-defense. The Motts decided they themselves would never resort to violence. But they questioned whether they could reasonably expect the same behavior of blacks who had spent their lives within the vicious system of slavery, which was now being enforced by a federal law.

Lucretia continued to act on her belief that moral reform was the best means of correcting injustice. She supported abolitionist John Brown's intention to free the slaves, but she disapproved of the violent methods he employed. Brown's ultimate effort took place in 1859, when with a band of 18 men, he attacked the federal arsenal at Harpers Ferry, Virginia, in hopes of inciting a slave revolt. Ten raiders and seven defenders were killed. Captured by federal troops, Brown was ultimately convicted and hanged. During his controversial trial, Brown's wife, Mary Ann, received comfort and support from the Motts, who had invited her to stay at their home in Philadelphia. Although John Brown's attempt to free slaves had failed miserably, many abolitionists hailed him as a martyr.

When war between the North and the South broke out in 1861, Lucretia opposed it. However, she continued in her efforts to support basic human rights and justice.

Despite her advancing years, Lucretia Mott remained active in a multitude of causes. She worked to help newly freed slaves during the Civil War, and after the war supported suffrage for blacks and women. Mott also remained involved in the Pennsylvania Peace Society, serving as its president from 1870 until her death.

7

"MY WORK IS DONE"

Unlike some people who grow more conservative as they age, broad-minded Lucretia seemed to become even more liberal. Over the years, her daughters and granddaughters, too, became less strict about wearing excessively plain Quaker clothing— although none wore hoops—and even music and dancing were allowed in their homes. Lucretia was tolerant of their liberal lives, and she herself came to like music, particularly "Negro spirituals," the often religious songs sung by slaves and freed blacks.

Despite the Quaker stand against celebrating Christmas, when the holidays came, Lucretia baked pies and cookies for Civil War soldiers and for the black residents of the old age home and orphanage in Philadelphia. And although the Quakers also pro-hibited alcohol use, in her later years she drank small amounts of wine to settle her stomach.

Lucretia's stand on divorce was modified, too, when she witnessed the unhappy dissolution of a relative's marriage. In 1861, despite the onset of the Civil War, she traveled alone to a women's rights meeting in Albany, New York. While there, she, along with Elizabeth Cady Stanton and Ernestine Rose, addressed the New York State legislature. Before this distinguished company of men Lucretia let fly one of the most radical speeches ever heard on the subject of matrimony and government. According to her, marriage was a sacred union between two people only, and the law should have nothing to do with it. In fact, all laws governing both marriage and divorce should be eliminated. Soon after this address, Lucretia and James celebrated their 50th wedding anniversary; the two remained closer than ever.

During the Civil War Lucretia busied herself raising money and procuring clothes for the slaves freed by the advancing Union Army. At her Quaker Meeting, she helped found the Women's Association for the Aid of the Freedmen. Here she was amused to see that some of those who had been opposed to her active abolitionism were now involved in sewing and packing clothes and blankets for newly freed slaves.

But war intruded in the lives of pacifists when an 1863 federal law required that male citizens be drafted into service. Conscientious objectors—those who did not wish to serve in the armed forces because of moral or religious beliefs—had to request exemption from the draft. Lucretia did not hesitate to help those Quakers and others who were drafted. She publicly supported them and sometimes went with them to their hearings.

Lucretia's friends and family were not as opposed to the war as she might have liked. Elizabeth Cady Stanton and Susan B. Anthony formed the National Women's Loyal League to support the aims of the war (if not the fighting itself), and they put women's rights on the back burner for the time being. Lucretia did not join the organization, but she was present at its first meeting.

Since 1857, James and Lucretia had been living permanently at their farmhouse, Roadside, outside Philadelphia. Their daughter Marie and her husband, Edward Davis, owned the land next door. For the duration of the war, Edward leased his land to the

army. There, a camp for black soldiers was constructed and named, strangely enough, after the pacifist Quaker William Penn. Lucretia was heartened, despite her pacifism, by the presence of black soldiers in the war effort; they themselves would have a hand in the victory over slavery.

Lucretia visited the soldiers at Camp William Penn and brought food as well as words of encouragement. Her Roadside neighbors later remembered how Lucretia, at age 70, would dump her cookie jar into her apron and run out to the road to offer the treats to the soldiers marching by. Pacifism, to Lucretia, did not mean refraining from acts of kindness toward soldiers. (After the war Davis would sell parcels of his land to both blacks and whites, who would build houses there. One of the first integrated communities, the area would be named LaMott in Lucretia's honor.)

In 1863, Congress authorized the enlistment of black soldiers into the Union Army. As a Quaker, Lucretia Mott disapproved of war, but she supported the idea of blacks having the opportunity to participate equally in society as American soldiers.

Many of Lucretia's family members and friends were actively involved in the war effort. Miller McKim, the Wrights, and son-in-law Edward Davis abandoned their nonresistance position to support the war. Davis entered the service and was commissioned a captain under General John Fremont. (Fremont made it his policy to release slaves in the territories he captured—before it was government policy to do so. For these efforts, however, he was relieved of his command.) Lucretia's granddaughter, Maria Hopper, became a Civil War nurse. A grandson, Willie Wright, enlisted in the Union army. After he was wounded at Gettysburg in 1863, Willie was nursed back to health at Roadside.

In their day-to-day lives, both James and Lucretia witnessed the prejudice that kept black Americans from achieving full equality. The horse-drawn streetcars that ran from Philadelphia to the Motts' neighborhood, which included Camp William Penn, were segregated. Blacks could ride only in designated cars, and if those were full, they had to ride outside. Several times both James and Lucretia—now over 70—fell ill after riding outside in cold and wet weather with the banished people. The Quaker group Friends Association for the Aid and Elevation of the Freedmen appointed the Motts to a committee to do something about the segregation between blacks and whites on streetcars. A few years later their efforts succeeded.

The end of the Civil War in 1865 was cause for rejoicing, but sorrow followed a few days later with the assassination of President Abraham Lincoln. Lucretia allowed her son-in-law to drape black bunting on Roadside's porch, even though such a display was not in line with Lucretia's Quakerism. Lucretia's daughter Elizabeth also died that year at Roadside. Despite her own and James's failing health, Lucretia had nursed their daughter throughout her decline from cancer.

Lucretia's belief that the war would not resolve the problems caused by slavery was borne out at the end of the war. The true root of inequality, she preached, was a lack of civil rights. The slaves were free, but they still suffered from poverty and a lack of skills, resources, and equality under the law. Accordingly, Lucretia and James continued their activism by raising money to help freed men and women begin anew, to educate themselves and their children, and to learn trades.

The following year brought more activity and more struggle. James was elected president of the Pennsylvania Peace Society, a new organization that strove to prevent armed conflict, or indeed conflict of any kind.

Shortly after this meet-ing, Elizabeth Cady Stanton, Susan B. Anthony, and Lucy Stone formed the American Equal Rights Associ-ation. The purpose of the organization was to gain the vote for both blacks and women. Lucretia was the nominal president, but she relied heavily, by previous agreement, on her vice president, Elizabeth Cady Stanton. Lucretia was looking for younger activists to step forward and take her place in the women's rights struggle. Over the next three years, differences of opinion within the reform movement would often make Lucretia ill. As a result, she was finally willing on occasion to turn down the endless requests for her support.

Susan B. Anthony (right) and Elizabeth Cady Stan-ton believed that suffrage should be granted to blacks and to women at the same time. In 1866, they formed the American Equal Rights Association, with Lucretia Mott as president, dedi-cated to this goal of universal suffrage.

When members of the American Equal Rights Association voted in 1869 to support the not-yet-ratified Fifteenth Amendment, which granted suffrage for blacks but not for women, Stanton and Anthony resigned. They formed the National Woman Suffrage Association (NWSA), whose goal was the passage of a constitutional amendment granting women the right to vote.

Still, when her health allowed, Lucretia remained active. One anecdote in particular conveys the endurance she still had in her seventies: Lucretia continued to travel alone and often went into Philadelphia on charitable errands or shopping trips. The horse-drawn streetcar line ended a mile from Roadside, and if James Mott or a hired hand was not there to pick her up, she walked. Once she had picked up a secondhand highchair on her way home from the city, but found no one to meet her at the end of the line. So she took off her bonnet, rested the highchair on her head, and in this manner walked home across the fields.

In 1867, Lucretia attended the annual Anti-Slavery Society meeting in New York. Then she presided over that year's American Equal Rights Association meeting. The group was increasingly divided over the newly proposed Fourteenth Amendment, which guaranteed the full rights of citizenship to freed slaves, but defined these citizens and voters as male.

Lucretia continued to advocate suffrage for all

adults—black or white, male or female. In the new amendment's present form, Stanton and Anthony did not support it. But they worked tirelessly, trying to have its wording changed to ensure the right to vote for all citizens, male and female. But other leaders told the women it was "the Negroes' hour"—that they should stop shifting the focus to women. Even Frederick Douglass, who had supported the first public women's rights convention at Seneca Falls, remarked:

> When women, because they are women, are hunted down through the cities of New York and New Orleans; when they are dragged from their houses and hung from lamp posts; when their children are torn from their arms, and their brains bashed out upon the pavement, when they are objects of insult and outrage at every turn, when they are in danger of having their homes burnt down over their heads, when their children are not allowed to enter schools; then they will have an urgency to obtain the ballot equal to our own.

Lucretia feared that if the amendment failed to include women now, it would be a long time before the injustice was corrected. She solidly supported the rights of black men to vote. However she thought that women "had the right to be a little jealous of the addition of so large a number of men to the voting class, for the colored men would naturally throw all their strength on the side of those opposed to woman's enfranchisement." Lucretia could hardly oppose the amendment's purpose, though, as she had spent her life working to obtain freedom and full rights for slaves.

In January 1868, while the Motts were in New York attending a wedding, James fell ill with a cold. It turned to pneumonia, and at the end of the month he died, surrounded by his loving family. The Mott children feared their mother, after 56 years of steady companionship and support, might not want to live without her beloved James. Despite her deep sorrow, however, Lucretia did find the will to live on, and after several

Lucy Stone (above), along with Henry Blackwell and Julia Ward Howe, established the American Woman Suffrage Association (AWSA). Although the NWSA and AWSA had the same goal—obtaining a woman's right to vote—the two organizations would not work together for another 21 years.

months of mourning, she regained some of her energy.

Lucretia was increasingly dismayed by the deepening rifts in the women's rights movement. When Lucy Stone and Julia Howe formed the New England Woman Suffrage Association, Lucretia refused to attend its convention because the organizers had pointedly excluded Susan B. Anthony and Elizabeth Cady Stanton. But Lucretia was disappointed in these old comrades too, because they had accepted the support of a Democratic politician who was strongly prejudiced against blacks.

In May 1869 Lucretia again chaired the American Equal Rights Association meeting in New York. Its members were torn between suffragists who opposed the newly passed Fifteenth Amendment, which specifically gave the right to vote to blacks, and suffragists who supported the amendment, feeling "half a loaf" was better than none. Immediately after the meeting, Stanton and Anthony resigned from the organization, and formed the National Woman Suffrage Association. Their opponents, Lucy Stone and her supporters, formed the American Woman Suffrage Association. The divisions between these old friends and other reformers such as Frederick Douglass again placed Lucretia in the role of peacemaker. She was glad to continue north for a visit to Nantucket after the tumultuous sessions.

In late 1869, however, came a more pleasant task. Lucretia was happy to participate in the opening ceremonies of Swarthmore College, a coeducational Quaker (Hicksite) school for which she and James had worked for many years to raise money. Today the school serves as a repository for many of Lucretia's letters and other personal papers.

Early the next year, Lucretia was dealt another blow when her sister Eliza died. The two women had spent almost their entire lives together, and the loss of this favorite sister was difficult. To distract herself from this grief, Lucretia decided to attend and speak at every black church in Philadelphia, as a "parting legacy," she said, "having long mourned with those who mourned, now to rejoice with those who do rejoice."

The next month the Fifteenth Amendment, which specifically extends the right to vote to black men, was ratified by the states and became law. Lucretia's fears were borne out—50 more years would pass before another amendment declared that women could vote in all U.S. elections. Nevertheless, she celebrated the passage of the Fifteenth Amendment as a victory that crowned the Motts' long antislavery struggle. Later in 1870, the Philadelphia Female Anti-Slavery Society and others like it were disbanded, although Lucretia and other reformers knew that the fight against inequality was far from finished.

In April 1870 Lucretia agreed to negotiate between the two quarreling groups in the women's rights movement. However, she did not succeed: "I went not expecting great things and I didn't get 'em—Glad to be out of it all, and I never meant to join another organization," she wrote a friend afterward.

For several years she tried to remain uninvolved in women's rights issues. She did continue to work for other causes, albeit less frequently, by supporting the Northern Association for the Relief of Poor Women and helping freed slaves. She packed clothes and farm produce to send to the poor, and she helped raise money for schools.

But the endless requests for her to support various reform organizations kept coming. Son-in-law Edward Davis answered the mail that poured in from across the country. Lucretia now enjoyed—or suffered from—a fame that resembled veneration. "I'm a much over-rated woman, it's humiliating," she remarked.

Still, despite her poor health—she was now in her eighties and weighed only 80 pounds—she insisted on traveling alone and kept up as much as she could with her old friends and causes. In the month of May alone, she attended the Quaker Yearly Meeting, the Quaker Quarterly Meeting, the last Anti-Slavery Society meeting, a graduation ceremony at the Female Medical College, the Pennsylvania Peace Society's meeting, and another meeting for freed slaves.

The cause that replaced antislavery in the forefront of Lucretia's heart in these later years was the one for peace. She served as president of the Pennsylvania Peace Society from 1870 until her death, and she preached against war as much as she had once preached against slavery. She continued to travel—to cities in New York, Massachusetts, and Pennsylvania— and even went on an unannounced, uninvited visit to a neighbor's house to see President Ulysses S. Grant, who was visiting.

In 1874, however, Lucretia suffered a string of heartbreaking events with the deaths of several people with whom she had been close. Family friend Miller McKim, daughter Anna Hopper, grandson Isaac Hopper, and sister Martha Wright all died that year. Lucretia herself began to prepare for her own end—which actually would not come for several more years.

Lucretia remained active, still accepting invitations to speak: at the Pennsylvania Abolition Society in 1875; at the Mother's Day celebration a month later, and again the next year; and at a meeting of the National Woman Suffrage Association in Philadelphia on the country's centennial, July 4, 1876. At these appearances she often received standing ovations merely by being introduced.

At the 1876 National Woman Suffrage Association meeting Lucretia actually presided, standing for four hours straight. One newspaper report quoted the "farewell speech" that she gave, in which she told the

assembly how to respond to the news of her death: "Weep not for me. Rather let your tears flow for the sorrows of the multitude. My work is done. . . . Death has no terrors, for it is a wise law of nature. I am ready whenever the summons may come."

Later that year, the frail 83-year-old again visited her birthplace, taking a granddaughter and several great-granddaughters to see the sites of her childhood. It would be her last visit to Nantucket.

In 1878 Lucretia traveled to Rochester, New York, to celebrate the 30th anniversary of the Seneca Falls convention. Here, too, she received a standing ovation and a tribute from Frederick Douglass.

If long trips were becoming fewer and farther between during Lucretia's last years, short ones were not. She attended the Pennsylvania Peace Society meetings and some Quaker Meetings in Philadelphia throughout the late 1870s. At the former, she chaired most meetings. In 1879, too, Lucretia continued to

At an 1869 inaugural celebration at Swarthmore College, one of its founders, Lucretia Mott, helps plant a tree on the school grounds.

Roadside, located in the community of Chelten Hills, outside Philadelphia, was Lucretia Mott's home from 1857 until her death in 1880, at the age of 87.

attend Fourth-Day (as Quakers call Thursday) Meetings in Philadelphia, despite her increasingly poor health.

At the 1879 Quaker Yearly Meeting in November, the 86-year-old reformer was accompanied by her daughter Maria, who reported that "it was an ovation every day, in the multitude which came just to take her by the hand. . . . [T]he only way to escape this, for it was very exhausting, was to leave before the closing minute was read." Lucretia was even lionized by the New York Quaker Meeting, which had been hostile to her in decades past. Maria noted a remark she had overheard in Meeting one day: "Lucretia has outlived all her persecutors."

If Lucretia was disappointed that none of her children and few grandchildren were Quakers anymore, she did not show it. Similarly, none of her children and grandchildren were actively involved in reform efforts. The women in her family seemed content to be wives and mothers—and this too was fine with Lucretia:

"Like Elizabeth Cady Stanton," biographer Margaret Hope Bacon surmises, "[Lucretia] may have made up her mind that her descendants in reform would be the men and women she had inspired rather than those to whom she had given birth."

By 1880, Lucretia found she lacked the energy and strength to venture far from her house. The stream of visitors to Lucretia's home slowed down, but it never really ceased. Susan B. Anthony, William Lloyd Garrison, and other old friends made several trips to see her at Roadside.

In the fall of that year, she began to fail more each day, gradually and without complaint. The word spread among friends and family that they needed to say good-bye. As she spoke with her family, she urged them to keep her funeral simple, to reflect the Quaker values she had espoused throughout her life.

On November 11, 1880, Lucretia Mott died, surrounded by all her surviving children and grandchildren. She was memorialized, as she wished, in a simple ceremony at Roadside. Then her small coffin was taken to the cemetery where several thousand had silently gathered. One colleague spoke and then there was silence.

"Will no one speak?" someone asked.

Another answered, "Who can speak? The preacher is dead."

CHRONOLOGY

1793   Lucretia Coffin born in Nantucket, Massachusetts, on January 3 to Anna and Thomas Coffin

1804   Coffin family moves to Boston, Massachusetts

1806   Attends Quaker boarding school, Nine Partners, located in New York

1808   Completes studies at Nine Partners; accepts teaching position there

1810   Leaves Nine Partners and with family moves to Philadelphia, Pennsylvania

1811   Marries James Mott in Philadelphia

1817   Becomes seriously ill, as does her son Thomas Coffin Mott; Thomas dies

1818   Speaks in Quaker Meeting for the first time; on a visit to Virginia witnesses slavery firsthand

1821   Named a minister of the Quaker faith

1830   Chosen as clerk of the Philadelphia Women's Yearly Meeting

1833   Preaches at Nantucket; assists with the first National Anti-Slavery Convention held in Philadelphia; founds the Philadelphia Female Anti-Slavery Society

1837   Attends the first Anti-Slavery Convention of American Women in New York City

1838   Pennsylvania Hall burned by angry mob during second Anti-Slavery Convention of American Women, held in Philadelphia

1840   With husband James, attends World Anti-Slavery Convention held in London, but women are not admitted as delegates; travels throughout Delaware, Pennsylvania, and New Jersey to preach and speak against slavery

1842   Travels through Maryland and Virginia speaking with slaveholders about abolition

1843   Gives a speech in Washington, D.C., that is attended by many congressmen; for the first time her Meeting denies its support of her preaching; she continues regardless

1844   Becomes seriously ill; mother, Anna Coffin, dies; founds the Association for the Relief of Poor Women

1847   Speaks at the New England Anti-Slavery Society meeting in Boston; with James Mott, travels to Quaker Meetings in Ohio and Indiana

1848 With James, attends the Anti-Sabbath Convention in Boston; helps organize first public women's rights meeting: the Seneca Falls convention

1849 Gives famous speech "Discourse on Woman"

1852 Presides over a national woman's rights convention in Syracuse, New York

1865 President Abraham Lincoln is assassinated; daughter Elizabeth dies

1866 With James, becomes active in the Pennsylvania Peace Society and the American Equal Rights Association

1868 Husband James Mott dies

1870 The Fifteenth Amendment is ratified and becomes law; the Philadelphia Female Anti-Slavery Society disbands; becomes president of the Pennsylvania Peace Society

1876 Attends the U.S. centennial celebrations in Philadelphia on July 4; visits Nantucket for the last time

1878 Travels to Rochester, New York, to celebrate the 30th anniversary of the Seneca Falls convention

1880 Dies at her home, Roadside, on November 11

1776	Abigail Adams asks husband John to "remember the Ladies" when formulating the new nation's government; the U.S. Declaration of Independence states that "all men are created equal"
1821	Emma Hart Willard founds the Troy Female Seminary in New York, which is the first school of higher education for women
1833	Oberlin College, Ohio, is the first college to open its doors to men and women, black and white
1836	Angelina and Sarah Grimké begin speaking publicly against slavery
1837	First Anti-Slavery Convention of American Women held in New York City; Mary Lyon founds Mount Holyoke College, first four-year college for women only
1839	American Anti-Slavery Society votes to allow women within its organization; Mississippi passes the first Married Woman's Property Act
1840	World Anti-Slavery Convention held in London; women delegates are not allowed to participate
1844	First labor association for women—Lowell Female Labor Reform Association—established in Massachusetts
1848	At first public convention on women's rights, in Seneca Falls, New York, participants sign a Declaration of Sentiments and Resolutions that lists women's grievances
1849	Escaped slave Harriet Tubman leads first of many groups of slaves to freedom via the Underground Railroad
1850	Female Medical College of Pennsylvania opens its doors
1851	At women's rights convention in Ohio, Sojourner Truth delivers "Ain't I a Woman?" speech
1852	Harriet Beecher Stowe publishes *Uncle Tom's Cabin*, an immediate best-seller that shapes the nation's attitude toward slavery
1861–65	American Civil War effectively halts suffrage activity for women
1866	Elizabeth Cady Stanton, Susan B. Anthony, and Lucy Stone found the American Equal Rights Association
1869	The women's rights movement splits; Susan B. Anthony and Elizabeth Cady Stanton form the National Woman Suffrage Association (NWSA); Lucy Stone, Henry Blackwell, and Julia Ward Howe organize the American Woman Suffrage Association (AWSA)

THE ROAD TO WOMEN'S RIGHTS IN THE UNITED STATES

1870	Fifteenth Amendment is ratified, giving vote to black men but not women
1872	Susan B. Anthony is arrested for voting; she hopes the arrest will lead to a trial in which the wording of the Fourteenth Amendment will be interpreted as guaranteeing women the right to vote
1875	The U.S. Supreme Court rules the Fourteenth Amendment does not apply to women
1878	A woman suffrage amendment is introduced in the U.S. Congress but does not pass
1884	Belva Lockwood, the first female lawyer to practice before the U.S. Supreme Court, runs for president on National Equal Rights Party ticket
1890	The NWSA and AWSA unite as the National American Woman Suffrage Association (NAWSA)
1891	Ida B. Wells initiates nationwide antilynching campaign after three black businessmen are murdered in Memphis, Tennessee
1893	Colorado becomes the first state to adopt a state amendment giving women the right to vote
1896	National Association of Colored Women (NACW) is formed in Washington, D.C.; first large woman suffrage march is held in New York City
1903	Women's Trade Union League of New York established; group works for unionization of working women and for suffrage
1909–10	The largest strike of women workers is held, predominantly in New York among shirtwaist makers
1915	Suffragists gather more than half a million signatures on petitions to present to Congress; 40 thousand march in New York City
1916	Jeanette Rankin of Montana becomes first woman elected to U.S. House of Representatives
1919	Nineteenth Amendment, guaranteeing women's right to vote in every state and federal election, passes House and Senate and goes to states for ratification
1920	The Nineteenth Amendment is ratified; NAWSA organization now becomes League of Women Voters

THE ROAD TO WOMEN'S RIGHTS IN THE UNITED STATES

1933	Frances Perkins appointed secretary of labor by President Franklin D. Roosevelt, becoming the first woman to hold a cabinet position
1941–45	Women begin performing "men's" jobs in factories when United States enters World War II
1953	Oveta Culp Hobby becomes first woman secretary of health, education, and welfare
1964	Civil Rights Act of 1964 passes, prohibiting discrimination by gender in employment
1968	Shirley Chisholm is first black woman elected to U.S. House of Representatives
1972	Civil Rights Act passes, prohibiting discrimination by sex in education; Equal Rights Amendment (ERA) is passed and sent to states for ratification
1977	First National Women's Conference, organized in part by Bella Abzug, is held in Houston, Texas
1980	Census Bureau allows for first time that women can be "heads of household"
1981	Sandra Day O'Connor is first woman appointed to U.S. Supreme Court
1982	The ERA falls three states short of ratification
1984	Geraldine Ferraro becomes first female vice presidential candidate nominated by a major political party; runs on Democratic ticket with Walter Mondale
1986	U.S. Supreme Court rules that sexual harassment constitutes sex discrimination and is therefore illegal
1993	Janet Reno becomes first female U.S. attorney general; Carol Mosley-Braun is first black woman to serve in U.S. Senate
1996	Madeleine Albright becomes first female U.S. secretary of state

FURTHER READING

Bacon, Margaret Hope. *Valiant Friend: The Life of Lucretia Mott*. New York: Walker & Company, 1980.

————. *Mothers of Feminism: The Story of Quaker Women in America*. New York: Harper & Row, 1986.

Cromwell, Otelia. *Lucretia Mott*. Cambridge, Mass.: Harvard University Press, 1958.

Davis, Lucile. *Lucretia Mott*. Mankato, Minn.: Bridgestone Books, 1998.

Fritz, Jean. *You Want Women to Vote, Lizzie Stanton?* New York: G. P. Putnam's Sons, 1995.

Greene, Dana, ed. *Lucretia Mott: Her Complete Speeches and Sermons*. New York: Edwin Mellen Press, 1980.

Kalman, Bobbie. *Nineteenth Century Girls and Women*. New York: Crabtree Publishing, 1997.

Nash, Carol Rust. *The Story of the Women's Movement*. Chicago, Ill.: Children's Press, 1989.

Sawyer, Kem Knapp. *Lucretia Mott: Friend of Justice*. Lowell, Mass.: Discovery Enterprises, 1991.

Swain, Gwyneth. *The Road to Seneca Falls: A Story About Elizabeth Cady Stanton*. Minneapolis, Minn.: Carolrhoda Books, 1996.

Weisberg, Barbara. *Susan B. Anthony*. New York: Chelsea House, 1988.

Yolen, Jane. *Friend: The Story of George Fox and the Quakers*. New York: Seabury Press, 1972.

INDEX

PICTURE CREDITS

Gina De Angelis earned her B.A. in theater and history at Marlboro College, Vermont, and her M.A. in history at the University of Mississippi. She is the author of several young adult books in history, biography, and other subjects. She has lived in Australia, performed at the Pennsylvania Renaissance Faire, and written drama as well as nonfiction. Gina lives in Williamsburg, Virginia, with her daughter and their beloved elderly gerbils, Frito and Je Ne Sais Quoi.

Matina S. Horner was president of Radcliffe College and associate professor of psychology and social relations at Harvard University. She is best known for her studies of women's motivation, achievement, and personality development. Dr. Horner has served on several national boards and advisory councils, including those of the National Science Foundation, Time Inc., and the Women's Research and Education Institute. She earned her B.A. from Bryn Mawr College and her Ph.D. from the University of Michigan, and holds honorary degrees from many colleges and universities, including Mount Holyoke, Smith, Tufts, and the University of Pennsylvania.